The NCTE High Schoc

Sandra Cisneros in the Classroom

"Do not forget to reach"

The NCTE High School Literature Series

Carol Jago

Santa Monica High School

NATIONAL COUNCIL OF TEACHERS OF ENGLISH
1111 W. KENYON ROAD, URBANA, ILLINOIS 61801-1096

We gratefully acknowledge Susan Bergholz Literary Services, who generously gave us permission to reproduce the following material:

"Abuelito Who," "Good Hotdogs," "Peaches—Six in a Tin Bowl, Sarajevo," and "His Story." From MY WICKED WICKED WAYS. Copyright © 1987 by Sandra Cisneros, published by Third Woman Press and in hardcover by Alfred A. Knopf. Reprinted by permission of Susan Bergholz Literary Services, New York. All rights reserved.

Cover photo by Diana Solís. Reprinted with permission.

Staff Editor: Bonny Graham
Interior Design: Jenny Jensen Greenleaf
Cover Design: Jenny Jensen Greenleaf and Tom Jaczak

NCTE Stock Number: 42311-3050
ISSN 1525-5786

© 2002 by the National Council of Teachers of English.

Library of Congress Cataloging-in-Publication Data
Jago, Carol, 1951–
     Sandra Cisneros in the classroom : "do not forget to reach" / Carol Jago.
          p. cm. — (The NCTE high school literature series, ISSN 1525-5786)
Includes bibliographical references.
     ISBN 0-8141-4231-1
     1. Cisneros, Sandra—Study and teaching (Secondary) 2. Mexican Americans in literature—Study and teaching (Secondary) I. Title. II. Series.
     PS3553.I78 Z74 2002
     818' .5409—dc21
                                                                    2001008209

I have suspected for a long time now that our job as Chicanos, as *mexico-americanos*, as amphibians, as citizens with one foot over there and one over here, is to be the bridge of unity, to be the translator in this new age, *el sexto sol*, this age of chaos in which we are living when one world ends and a new one begins.

—Sandra Cisneros

Contents

■ ■

When a writer wants you to know that she is nobody's mother
and nobody's wife, you can safely assume this is a person of
considerable style and attitude. Sandra Cisneros is both and
has both. This chapter provides background information about
Cisneros's life and ideas to help students write about their own
childhood experiences.

Cisneros's poems provide powerful models for student writing. This
chapter includes Sandra Cisneros's poem "Abuelito Who" and offers
a sample lesson using poetry writing as a vehicle for teaching
students how to read poetry.

As well as being a writer, Sandra Cisneros is a writing teacher.
This chapter includes ideas that Cisneros has shared with
audiences in answer to the ubiquitous question, "How do you do
it?" It offers a sample lesson for teaching sensory imagery using
Cisneros's poem "Good Hotdogs" as well as an interview with the
author by Renée Shea.

The NCTE High School Literature Series

Apart from Emily Dickinson, Walt Whitman, Langston Hughes, and Mark Twain, few writers stand out as individuals in students' minds. Why should they? Teenagers seldom read multiple works by a single author (apart from Stephen King and Michael Crichton, of course) and even more rarely works by one writer across genres. The reason has partly to do with the way we design instruction. More often than not, teachers serve students a smorgasbord of poems and stories, hoping that one will pique their appetite for more. Rather than developing a deep knowledge of a particular writer's work, students emerge with the vague sense that some poems and stories are "pretty cool" while others are "boring." This is not the kind of experience that makes for lifelong lovers of literature.

Another way to organize a literature curriculum is around the in-depth study of individual writers. When students read a collection of poems, essays, or stories by one author, written over many years and in a variety of moods and historical moments, they begin to determine for themselves what is unique about a writer, what makes him or her worthy of the exalted title, "artist." Students journey into the minds of these artists and begin to consider how writers' lives sometimes shape what they produce. You might compare these two kinds of literature study with the difference between having many acquaintances or a small, close group of friends. I know which I would choose every time.

As a classroom teacher working in a public urban high school, I understand firsthand the challenges involved in teaching literature to today's students. One-third of the students at Santa Monica High School are English-language learners. There are over thirty different languages spoken on campus. Ethnically, the campus is a mirror of California, a state where no one group can claim a majority. In Los Angeles, Latinos have replaced whites as the largest ethnic group. Our student body includes children who live in million-dollar homes and others who reside in homeless shelters. Whatever their backgrounds and home lives, video games and television compete for their reading time, and too often books lose.

For many students, the only books they have read are the ones I put in their hands. These teenagers need powerful stories and poems to engage them, but pulling them away from their screens is hard work. This series offers a way to break through to kids. Since popular culture has conditioned young people to be enamored of the cult of personality, I invite them to explore the life, work, and personality of writers such as Nikki Giovanni, Alice Walker, and Sandra Cisneros, outrageous and outspoken individuals whose struggles and stories resonate with students' own experiences. As they read deeply of a single writer's work, they develop confidence and begin to have views about novels and poems that are as authoritative and important to them as their views on movies and music.

My students have grown attached to the authors in this series. I think yours will, too.

CAROL JAGO
Santa Monica High School
Santa Monica, California

Introduction

■ ■

Sandra Cisneros's stories have changed the world. An outrageous assertion? Maybe. But reflecting on the impact *The House on Mango Street* has had on students at my high school over the past decade, I have come to believe that one slim volume can indeed alter our angle of repose.

In 1985 our school librarian stopped me as I rushed through the main office and crammed a colorful little paperback into the pile I was carrying. "Carol, take a look at this. I know you're always looking for multicultural books." I thanked her and dashed off. The bell would ring in five minutes and it was reading day. I needed to be poised behind a student desk when kids arrived, modeling the kind of behavior I expected from them. *The House on Mango Street* happened to be in my hand, so I turned to page one without knowing a thing about the book or about this new young writer.

"We didn't always live on Mango Street. Before that we lived on Loomis on the third floor, and before that we lived on Keeler. Before Keeler it was Paulina, and before that I can't remember" (1). Within seconds I was captivated by the rhythm of Cisneros's language. I can't remember how obediently my students read during the following fifty minutes, because I never looked up. I do remember that as I turned the last page the bell rang. I immediately began shouting to the class that they all needed to read this book, now! This minute! Hurry, who wants it next? (Over time my students become accustomed to such outbursts and agree to borrow the book I'm thrusting in their direction lest I explode.)

That was the start of my own personal obsession with putting *The House on Mango Street* into English teachers' and students' hands. It took a few years—English departments move with glacial speed—but we finally incorporated Cisneros's collection into our ninth-grade curriculum, where it has lived ever since.

Coupling this title with traditional ninth-grade texts has shifted the balance of power in the curriculum. Maybe not more than a few degrees, but it has nonetheless shifted. Who could possibly have greater expectations than Esperanza? "One day I will pack my bags of books and paper. One day I will say goodbye to Mango. I am too strong for her to keep me here forever. One day I will go away" (110). Like Pip, Esperanza refuses to be defined by the circumstances that surround her. Like Charles Dickens, Sandra Cisneros offers readers a fictional world so rich in detail that we know what it feels like to walk down Paulina and to sit on those tight little steps. Pairing these two stories about young people in search of themselves sends students the subtle message that they, too, will one day have to set out on their own journey to self-discovery. Though Victorian London and the West Side of Chicago may look very different from one another and from the world in which our students live, the protagonist's dilemma remains the same. Male or female, British or Latino, prosperous or poor, for the struggling hero the world is a cruel place occasionally populated with the kindest of strangers.

Many of my students identify with both the fictional Esperanza, whose name means "hope," and with Sandra Cisneros. After reading *The House on Mango Street,* Lupe Ferreira, a young

woman who had recently been through a series of family trag-
edies, wrote:

> Believe in yourself
> In the power you have
> To control your own life
> Believe in tomorrow
> Let a hopeful heart carry you through

Sandra Cisneros's stories about Esperanza's life offered Lupe hope.
She wants to be a writer. That's what makes me say that Sandra
Cisneros has changed the world.

1 Where Life and Art Intersect

■■■■■■■■■■■■■■■■■■■■■■■■■■■■■■■■

Mining an author's life for nuggets of truth about her writing is always a dangerous business, but the autobiographical nature of Sandra Cisneros's work seems to invite such exploration. What makes any biographical study of Cisneros particularly problematic is the fact that she, thank goodness, is still a work in progress. I can't imagine what it would feel like to have scholars combing through the details of my childhood for fateful occurrences or foreshadowing of tragedy yet to come. I also can't imagine what it would be like to be identified as a role model for a generation of young Latinas. Finding a balance between public and private lives must be a constant struggle. Fortunately, Sandra Cisneros's generous heart has found room for her many readers.

> I am going to tell you a story about a girl who didn't want to belong.
> —Sandra Cisneros, *The House on Mango Street*

The Early Years

Sandra Cisneros was born in 1954 in Chicago. The only daughter in a family of six boys, she grew up in a bilingual, bicultural community. Her father was the son of a middle-class military man, while her mother grew up in poverty, first in Arizona and later in Chicago. "I grew up with a Chicana mother and a Mexican father, and we spoke English to her and Spanish to him" (Benson).

Cisneros's childhood in Chicago was often interrupted by summer trips to her grandfather's home in Mexico. While these trips offered a welcome respite from cold winters and crowded apartment living, they also created instability in her life. The family would "let go our flat, store the furniture with mother's relatives, load the station wagon with baggage and bologna sandwiches and head south" ("Ghosts and Voices" 69). On their return to Chicago weeks or months later, the family would move into one more apartment in yet another run-down neighborhood. The children would be enrolled in one more Catholic school to take up their U.S. lives where they had left off.

This early movement between cultures made Cisneros acutely aware of what it meant to live between two cultures. She often felt like an outsider in both places. Though she looked like a native in Mexico, she knew she was merely a visitor on a circumscribed vacation. Chicago, where she looked so different from the images on television and spoke a "foreign" language at home, was her family's home. Over time, Cisneros came to understand the cultural richness of living in two worlds, but as a child she lived with many contradictions. In the vignette "Those Who Don't" from *The House on Mango Street,* Esperanza—her fictional self— explains, "All brown all around, we are safe. But watch us drive into a neighborhood of another color and our knees go shakity-shake and our car windows get rolled up tight and our eyes look straight" (28).

Being the only girl in a family of boys further isolated Cisneros. Her traditional Mexican father believed that "daughters were meant for husbands" (Rodriguez Aranda 68). Her brothers paired off and for the most part left her to dream on her own. "These three sets of men had their own conspiracies and allegiances, leaving me the odd-woman-out forever" ("Ghosts and Voices," 69). Cisneros credits her feisty mother with giving her the courage to break through traditional barriers to create a life outside the boundaries that ethnicity and gender seemed to dictate as her future.

Cisneros has called her own education in Chicago's public schools "rather shabby" (Chavez 99) and often shares with groups of schoolchildren stories about her fifth-grade report card. "I had C's and D's in everything. . . . The only B I had was in conduct. But I don't remember being that stupid" (Tabor). In school she considered herself more of a reader than a writer, but in high school she began writing poems and editing the Josephium High School literary magazine. It was during this period that Cisneros began to consider the possibility of becoming a writer.

> I don't know when I first said to myself I am going to be a writer. Perhaps that first day my mother took me to the public library when I was five, or perhaps again when I was in high school and my English teacher forced me to read a poem out loud and I became entranced with the sounds, or perhaps when I enrolled in that creative writing class in college, not knowing it would lead to other creative writing workshops and graduate school. ("Notes to a Young[er] Writer")

In 1972 Sandra Cisneros enrolled at Loyola University in Chicago as an English major. With the encouragement of one of her professors, she applied and was accepted into the M.F.A. program at the prestigious University of Iowa Writers' Workshop. Cisneros described her experience at this famous institution in a 1986 lecture at Indiana University. The text of her speech, "Ghosts and Voices: Writing from Obsession," has been widely anthologized and is a must-read for anyone who works with young writers. In it she explains how she was able to stop writing what she thought others wanted and begin to write what she knew. "If I were asked what it is I write about, I would have to say I write about those ghosts inside that haunt me, that will not let me sleep, of that which even memory does not like to mention. Sometimes I am writing the same story, the same poem, over and over." It was during her time in the Iowa Workshop that Sandra Cisneros began writing the sketches that would later become *The House on Mango Street.*

Turning Students' Own Lives into Art

I often use Cisneros's essay "Ghosts and Voices: Writing from Obsession" to help me persuade students that their own childhood experiences are a rich source of material for writing. Like the young Cisneros, many believe that writing should be made of sterner stuff, serious subjects that exude insight and importance. As a result, they sit, pen in hand, paralyzed by the blank page.

To get those pens moving, I ask students to bring in a snapshot of themselves as small children. Any age will do, but most of the best writing has been inspired by photographs taken when the student was between the ages of four and ten. There's something about a baby picture that inspires foolishness rather than reflection. The photos that work best are often also of particular moments that students remember well: a disastrous birthday party, their first Holy Communion, holding a treasured pet or trophy, standing beside a beloved relative. It is sometimes a bit of a struggle to get a whole class to bring in a photo on the same day, so I announce the assignment a week ahead of time, which gives me four extra days of nagging before I actually begin the writing lesson. If for any reason a student has no pictures available, I simply tell him or her to use a student ID photo or driver's license.

I then show the class a black-and-white snapshot of me on the first day of fifth grade (see Figure 1.1). They laugh (with good reason), and I tell them what I remember of that day. I tell them how proud I was of my brand new pleated wool skirt—a hideous, long thing, scratchy and bright orange—and my new glasses with blue frames. I talk about how I remember that I had heard that the fifth-grade teacher was hard and mean, but that I was still glad school was starting. Mostly I remember a feeling of relief that a boring summer was finally over.

I then instruct students to look at their own photographs very carefully and record every detail they see and remember:

■ what they were wearing and how they remember feeling about these clothes

Figure 1.1 Carol Jago (then Crosetto) on the first day of school, 1961.

- the setting of the photograph, what time of year it was, what time of day
- who else is in the picture and the relationship of this person to themselves
- anything they might be holding or touching and what this object meant to them
- the reason the photo was taken and who took it
- their facial expression, what they were thinking at the time
- what they think or feel now as they look at their "former" self

After they've spent about fifteen minutes in intense observation, I tell them to show the photo to a partner and talk about it. Within a few seconds, the room explodes with stories and laughter. The photos act as windows to the world of their childhood, and most students find they have lots to say. Those who don't often ask for permission to bring in another picture they think would be "better." Of course!

The next day I have students bring out the photo again, and this time I ask them to write a letter to their younger self. I offer the following sample based on my own photo:

> Dear Carol,
>   Stop letting your mom cut your bangs. You look like a dork. Forget the pin curl perm at the sides, too. I know you think those glasses make you look cool, but you are wrong.
>   Stand up straight. Keep reading. And be nicer to your sister. Sometimes you can be insufferable.
>   Fondly,
>   Your grown-up self

Students find the letter format an easy one to follow and soon have a missive drafted. The purpose of this letter writing is to move students beyond simple description into reflection. I want their autobiographical pieces to be more than a retelling of a childhood incident; I'm hoping that their present self, as well as their child self, will be present in the piece. Such things have always seemed to me to be easier to inspire than to assign. We read a few of Sandra Cisneros's vignettes from *The House on Mango Street* and talk about how even though the narrator is the child Esperanza, we know that the writing hand is somehow her older self. I then ask students to write a vignette of their own based on a photograph.

Esmeralda Ruiz, a stylish and self-conscious tenth grader, brought in a picture of herself at five years old posing on her front lawn in a yellow bikini. She wrote:

Beauty Queen

Dreaming of Miss America, I practice smiling for the camera. The dry grass scratches my legs, but even at 5, I know that sometimes you need to suffer for beauty. Curly hair halos my little face. It's wispy like angel hair. Propped on an elbow, waiting for my mom to snap the picture, I smile my biggest smile. I am wearing my favorite bathing suit, a yellow string bikini framing a baby brown tummy. That day, I knew I was beautiful. Wish I felt that way every day.

A few students asked if they could write a poem instead, and I couldn't see why not, particularly given the poetic nature of Sandra Cisneros's prose. Like Esmeralda's vignette, Jason's poem "Tigers in the Backyard" seemed to strike just the balance I was hoping for between concrete description of a childhood scene and an awareness of the scene as memory:

Tigers in the Backyard

The four zones of the backyard:
The icy concrete court
The shady passageway
The wide open swing set grass
The wilderness behind the bushes

In the wilderness lurks
(I am sure)
wild Tigers
felines who crossed the Bering Strait
years ago to prowl in my backyard

"No one knows we're here"
they whisper as they hunt and roam
but they don't know that
I know their secret.
I know what to do.

With my new shovel,
I create a Tiger trap
It takes weeks to complete
Digging is hard
When the shovel is taller than you

Masked with dry leaves
The hole sat
And did what holes do
When they aren't catching Tigers

I never did catch a Tiger in my trap
Though I may have caused
The gardener to trip
Once or twice.

—Jason Kligier

Just as Sandra Cisneros found her writing voice when she began to write about what she knew, many of my students seem to find theirs when they write from childhood snapshots.

The Evolution of the Artist

After earning her M.F.A. from the University of Iowa, Cisneros returned to Chicago where she worked at the Latino Youth Alternative High School. She wrote about this teaching experience in the foreword to Gregory Michie's book *Holler If You Hear Me: The Education of a Teacher and His Students*. The last paragraph comparing learning to write with learning to teach struck me where I live.

> I was once a teacher of high school students. Back in 1977, fresh out of graduate school, I took a job teaching at an alternative high school on Chicago's South Side. It was a small school aimed primarily at returning "dropouts," although "dropout" didn't exactly fit their histories. Some of our kids were pushed out of school because they were parents. Some never went back because they were afraid of getting beat up by violent classmates. Some were with us because they had learning disabilities and were barely literate. Most had poor study skills and worse self-discipline habits that had contributed to their failure in the public schools. All of them wanted another chance at finishing their education in order to find a decent job.
>
> Even though I had minored in education and completed my student teaching in a Chicago public school, I wasn't prepared for my young students. After having spent 2 years in the Iowa Writers' Workshop listening to my classmates ramble on endlessly about meter and metaphor, it seemed incredible to be dealing daily with students who came to school with a black eye from a boyfriend or the calamity of another unwanted pregnancy. My kids had survived drive-by shootings; witnessed children robbing immigrants at gunpoint; saved their babies

from a third-floor flophouse fire by tossing them to neighbors below, then jumping; worked the night shift at a factory job they hated; run away from home and been homeless; hid the secret that they could not read; watched a father beat up their mother; drank and drugged themselves till they passed out; mothered three kids before they were eighteen; and a multitude of other outrageous experiences that would've made my Iowa Writers' Workshop classmates faint.

My students were not the greatest writers, but, man, could they talk a good story. They may have dropped out of high school, but they held doctorates from the university of life. They were streetwise and savvy; they were ingenuous and fragile. They had seen troubles the world's head of state would never see. In their short years on the planet they had lived extraordinary lives, and nobody had told them their lives were extraordinary, that they were extraordinary for having survived.

Needless to say, I made a lot of mistakes those first years. Eventually I came to realize that teaching was like writing. Just as I had to find my writing voice, I also had to find my teaching voice. They both came from my center, from my passions, from that perspective that was truly mine and made me different from any other teacher. To get there I had to take the same circular route as writing. I had to be intuitive, and I had to be willing to fail. (ix–x)

During this time, Cisneros continued to write and began giving readings as part of the Chicago Transit Authority's poetry project. In 1982 she received her first National Endowment for the Arts (NEA) grant, which allowed her to move to Massachusetts and complete *The House on Mango Street*. Published by Arte Público Press in 1984, the book met with rave reviews, receiving a Before Columbus Foundation American Book Award. It quickly became an underground classic and found its way into the syllabus of cultural studies courses at many universities. Mainstream readers, however, were unlikely to find the book at their local bookseller.

Cisneros then moved to San Antonio to take a job as arts administrator of the Guadalupe Arts Center. She felt much at home in this town where the cultures of Mexico and Texas blended. She felt that the

> landscape matches the one inside me, one foot in this country, one in that. . . . A place where two languages coexist, two cultures side by side. Not simply on street signs and condominiums. Not simply on menus and bags of chips. But in the public and private, sacred and profane, common and extraordinary circumstances of that homeland called the heart. (Jussawalla and Dasenbrock 298)

Unfortunately, the arts grants ran out and the economic reality of supporting herself forced Cisneros to leave San Antonio for a guest lectureship at California State University, Chico. There she struggled to find a balance between teaching and her own writing. Loving both, she could not find enough hours in the day to do both well. A second NEA fellowship allowed her to focus on her writing, and soon afterward she sold *Woman Hollering Creek* to Random House/Vintage, which also purchased the rights to and reprinted *The House on Mango Street*. *Woman Hollering Creek* is a collection of stories focusing on the lives of girls and women in the Latino community, strong females who struggle with the daily business of living in the barrio. Though each story can stand alone, the thread of strong women unites them. Cisneros's books were finally accessible to a wide audience of readers.

In 1991 *Woman Hollering Creek* won Cisneros the Lannan Literary Award for Fiction. Success with this collection and her book of poetry *My Wicked Wicked Ways* allowed her to move back to Texas. There she purchased her first home, a Victorian house in King Williams, a historic area near old San Antonio. When in

1997 she decided to paint the house bright purple, her neighbors were outraged. They felt Cisneros had violated the peaceful hue of their community. In her testimony before the King Williams Design Review Committee, Cisneros stated, "We don't exist. . . . [W]here is the visual record of our people[?] Are we to accept the version of the sleepy Mexican under the sombrero? . . . Are we only present in the food you like to eat? . . . Is our history to be told by the Daughters of the Republic of Texas?" The controversy reminded many of her loyal readers of the lines from *The House on Mango Street:*

> Not a flat. Not an apartment in back. Not a man's house. Not a daddy's. A house all my own. With my porch and my pillow, my pretty purple petunias. My books and my stories. My two shoes waiting beside the bed. Nobody to shake a stick at. Nobody's garbage to pick up after.
> Only a house quiet as snow. . . .(108)

In 1995 Cisneros received a MacArthur Foundation "genius grant," allowing her the financial freedom to continue to write and speak out on issues close to her heart. Through word and deed, she continues to inspire a generation of young writers and readers.

Further Resources

- An audiocassette of Sandra Cisneros reading *The House on Mango Street* is available from Random House (1998). I found it a lovely way to bring the author's voice into my classroom.
- Other poems that work well as models for writing from photographs are Raymond Carver's "On an Old Photograph of My Son" and "Photograph of My Father in His Twenty-second Year."

2 Writing from Models

In "Ghosts and Voices: Writing from Obsession," Sandra Cisneros describes the difficulty she had finding her voice when all of her models, all of the writers she admired, spoke in "big, male voices like James Wright and Richard Hugo and Theodore Roethke, all wrong for me" (70). Our students are more fortunate. They have Cisneros's stories and poems as models.

Getting inside a Poem

I often ask students to imitate published writers, not only for the finished work this produces but also for what students learn about the literature they imitate. Walking inside another writer's poem is one of the best ways I know of coming to understand its workings. Take, for example, Sandra Cisneros's poem about her grandfather, "Abuelito Who," from *My Wicked Wicked Ways*.

Abuelito Who
Sandra Cisneros

Abuelito who throws coins like rain
and asks who loves him
who is dough and feathers
who is a watch and glass of water
whose hair is made of fur
is too sad to come downstairs today
who tells me in Spanish you are my diamond
who tells me in English you are my sky

whose little eyes are string
can't come out to play
sleeps in his little room all night and day
who used to laugh like the letter k
is sick
is a doorknob tied to a sour stick
is tired shut the door
doesn't live here anymore
is hiding underneath the bed
who talks to me inside my head
is blankets and spoons and big brown shoes
who snores up and down up and down up and down again
is the rain on the roof that falls like coins
asking who loves him
who loves him who?

One of the things I have always loved best about this poem is Cisneros's use of metaphor. I do not, however, begin by telling students this. Instead, we read the poem aloud first and then silently. I ask students to choose a line that strikes them as interesting, odd, somehow luminous. (It's never a bad idea to use vocabulary you know many students won't know and then layer the meaning of the word into your explanation.) I tell them to underline the phrase and then write about it right on the page with the poem.

After about seven minutes, I begin calling on students to share the lines they've chosen and talk about what Cisneros's words made them see or feel. Because every—or almost every—student has something written on the page in front of him or her, I don't need to wait for volunteers. I purposely call on a student who rarely raises his or her hand. Often it is the same few students who volunteer and thus the same few voices that are heard. What is frustrating about this is that these hand raisers are not always the most thoughtful students, only the most confident. When I ask a student by name to share, my unspoken message is, "I know you are thinking. I'm sure you have something to say. You're smart, I can tell." Even if a student has blown off the last seven minutes combing her hair (not that anyone in your class would ever do such a thing), she can quickly glance down at the poem and come up with a line to talk about. In "Abuelito Who," almost any line will bear fruit. I also make it a classroom rule that students are not allowed to shrug and say, "Dunno." Instead they must reply, "Could you please come back to me? I'm still thinking." The unspoken assumption here is that everyone in the room is indeed thinking about the poem.

Even the roughest, most cursory response to a line is a start. It is an indication that students have begun to marshal their inchoate thoughts. What begins as a vague observation can develop into analysis. Before we begin talking, I read Cisneros's poem once more aloud.

Talking about a Poem

Ms. Jago: So, Deanna, what line did you underline?

Deanna: Well, I really liked "who is dough and feathers" because it made me think of the Pillsbury Doughboy and that's just what my grandfather feels like. The feathers part makes sense, too, because he's like a pillow.

Ms. Jago: Did you hear what you just said, "like a pillow"? Why do you think Sandra Cisneros didn't say, "who is like dough and feathers"?

Jorge: Well, like, it would be different then. I mean, when she says that he "is dough and feathers" I'm really seeing that gooey dough and feeling how soft those feathers are.

DEANNA: Yeah, I did, too, but I didn't get what she meant in the next line when she says he is a "glass of water."

JORGE: Oh, that's because he's sick. You know how sick people always have glasses of water by the bed. I guess they're always thirsty or something.

MS. JAGO: What about you, Dion? What line did you choose?

DION: "who used to laugh like the letter k" because I could just hear somebody who's sick laughing and kinda hacking at the same time. My grandpa smoked a lot and that's how he used to laugh. K,K,K, . . . [Dion imitates the sound, and of course all his buddies join in.]

MS. JAGO: Enough, we've got it. How about you, Jared? [to one of the cackling crowd]

JARED: I liked all the "who's." It just made the whole poem hang together or something. It's also a cool sound—"who, who, who, who, who." [The boys, of course, enter into this litany as well.]

DION: Yeah, that's good. And if she's talking about how her grandpa died and she can't stop thinking about him, the "who's" could be like this haunting sound. You know, "Whooooo. . . . Whoooooooo."

DEANNA: Where do you get that he's dead?

DION: Well, at the beginning it seems like she's a little girl always going into his bedroom, and then about halfway through the poem she says, "doesn't live here anymore." I know the next line is "is hiding under the bed," but I think that's not the real grandpa but like his ghost that she's afraid of. Real, sick grandpas don't crawl under the bed.

Ms. Jago: That's brilliant, Dion. For me the poem turns on exactly that line, "doesn't live here anymore." It's as though the first part is made of her memories of her grandfather when he was alive and the second part is how she feels about those memories as an adult.

Chris: Can I read what I wrote?

Ms. Jago: Of course.

Chris: "When you're a little kid old people don't quite seem real. They are just like what it says in this poem, 'blankets and spoons and big brown shoes'—a bunch of things that feel old and worn. They also smell."

Deanna: Hmmm. I wonder why she didn't write about smells. Chris is right.

I was delighted by the way students kept comparing the poem to their own experiences, testing the lines for authenticity. Early in this discussion I might have stopped students to talk about the difference between simile and metaphor in Cisneros's poem, but it just didn't seem right to interrupt the flow of their talk. Instead, I brought it up when we were ready to write poems like "Abuelito Who."

My instructions were simple:

Modeling Assignment

■ Reread Sandra Cisneros's poem at least three more times.

■ Think about a person who means a lot to you and whom you would like to write a poem about. This could be someone who will never be able to read this poem (someone who has died or a celebrity), or it might be someone in your life whom you might later choose to share your poem with. Pick someone you have strong feelings, either good or bad, for.

▪ Make a list of objects that remind you of this person. Choose concrete images—places, things, food, animals, household utensils. Instead of using a simile and writing, "Susie's eyes are like stars," do what Sandra Cisneros has done and state your comparisons as metaphors: "Marisol's eyes are stars. Marisol's hair is a jungle. Marisol is the Santa Monica Freeway."

▪ Using "Abuelito Who" as a model, turn your list into a poem. You might choose to title your poem "_____Who" as Cisneros has done.

I can't emphasize enough the importance of the first step. If students know a poem well, they will instinctively imitate its cadences, its tone, its pattern. This shouldn't be a fill-in-the-blanks assignment but rather an invitation to write in a particular poet's style. If a student asks to do something different (and someone invariably asks this question), I always say yes. Locking horns with a sixteen-year-old writer on this point is the quickest way to reinforce the student belief that I don't really care about what they have to say but only want things done "my way." Nine times out of ten, after being granted the right to write whatever he or she wants, the student decides to follow my instructions after all.

Typically we spend about half of a fifty-five-minute period talking about the model poem and then take about ten to fifteen minutes to write. Five minutes before the bell, I ask if anyone has a rough draft they would like to share. This, too, is an important step in the process because hearing how classmates have tackled an assignment helps those who are stuck see what they need to do for homework. We share quickly. As students listen to poems about ex-girlfriends, about dogs that have been run over, about Tupac Shakur, they often change their minds about the subjects they have chosen. I send them on their way with, I hope, a head full of ideas and a reminder that a revised, preferably typed poem is due the next day.

Which brings us to the thorny issue of homework.

Homework

"Homework! Oh, homework! / I hate you! You stink!" Children's poet Jack Prelutsky puts his finger on the one thing students worldwide agree on—homework stinks. From my vantage as a classroom teacher, nothing separates achieving students from those who make little progress more than the amount of time and effort they put into homework. Those who discipline themselves to complete at home the work that has begun in class tend to learn while the others languish.

There are, of course, a thousand reasons why teenagers don't do homework. Crowded conditions often make it difficult for students to find a quiet space for study. Many have jobs. Some have to care for younger siblings after school. On the other hand, I don't know a single student who doesn't manage to find time for television or talking on the phone. Teenagers make time for what is important to them. I believe we cheat students when we back away from holding them accountable for homework. If the assignment is meaningful and has been carefully constructed so that work begun in class can be completed at home, homework will deepen students' learning. It will also send them the message that literature doesn't belong only in school.

Invariably, when I start ranting about homework someone tells me to get off it, that homework is a middle-class notion, and that as long as I make out-of-class assignments a requirement for success, some students will be doomed to failure. I cannot accept this. While it may be true that many students face enormous obstacles to completing their homework, I refuse to solve the problem by not assigning it. Some educators have argued with me that assigning homework increases the differences between students from low-income and from affluent homes. I argue back that teachers at high-performing suburban schools are unlikely to stop assigning homework so that low-income students can catch up. If I want to work for greater equity, I need to find ways to make meaningful homework something all students get in the habit of completing.

Listening Like a Writer

When students arrive the next day with their revised poems in hand, I never have them simply pass the papers forward. Instead I ask them to turn to a partner and share what they've written. Sometimes the discomfort of admitting to a peer that they've done nothing since class yesterday is a better motivator than any subtraction of points or evil eye I might cast their way. Sometimes neither student has a paper to share. I tell these students to write while we go on with the lesson.

I remind the working pairs of students to listen like a writer; that is, to:

- give the reader your full attention
- offer a positive, encouraging comment first
- ask questions about references you don't understand
- let your partner know how the poem made you feel

As I describe what follows, it's important for you to know that I have between thirty-four and thirty-eight students enrolled in every class. California reduced class size in ninth grade to 20–1, but all other English classes are woefully overcrowded. Much of my classroom practice has grown out of finding ways to teach with so many bodies in the room. If I simply ask for volunteers to read their poems, we could take up the entire class period listening to a handful of poems. I need to make sure that every student who has written a poem has a chance to share that poem out loud to at least one other listener. Partner reading doesn't always work, and it doesn't always offer student writers the ideal feedback, but it is a way to ensure that all poems begin to live in another person's head.

After partners have worked together for about ten minutes, I ask if anyone has heard a poem that the rest of us need to hear. This simple question alters the dynamic of having students offer their own poems for classroom consumption. I want students to come up to the front of the class to read because along with making it easier for all to hear, it creates a sense of importance for the writer. They've worked on something that a classmate has said has value. The poem should in some way be showcased. I encourage readers to preface their poem with a short commentary. Listeners need a context for what they are about to hear. Invariably the funny or quirky poems are pushed forward first. We listen and laugh, and then make room in our heads for other sorts of poems.

Carrie was nervous about reading her poem. When her partner said she had to read "Jack Who," she pulled at her miniscule black skirt and pressed down on her dyed black bangs. After further prodding by teacher and peers, Carrie's knee-high motorcycle boots carried her reluctantly forward. She told us that this was a poem about her grandfather, who died of lung cancer when she was a little girl. I reminded her to look up, please, as she read.

Jack Who

Jack who is sweet rain
Asks me why he loves me so much
Who is Tupperware of fruit salad
and a gallon of fresh squeezed orange juice
Who is a book and a shell found on a white powdery beach
Whose hair is lost
And how he told me it just fell off
Whose voice is a comforting fire on a dreary day
Is too weak to go to breakfast this morning
Who is a gorilla
That escaped from his cage
Who tells me I'm his little gorilla
Who tells me from his temporary bed in Room 614
Not to go outside without a coat
Whose sky blue eyes are clouds
And streams
Watched TV all day and night
Who used to sit in silence at dinner parties
And the one word out of his mouth
Was the most important thing said all night
Can't breathe
Is always tied to a smoke
Is a tube in a machine
Lives in Room 614
Packaged orange juice
Whose bed is empty
Who I can still see in my dreams
Is a plaid shirt and pajamas and false teeth
Who coughs all day, all night
Is the symphony the rain makes
Telling me he loves me

—*Carrie Freiman*

Carrie's poem borrows heavily from Sandra Cisneros's "Abuelito Who" and yet remains her own creation. Cisneros's poem taught

Carrie how to collect what she remembered and then weave those memories into a poem. I don't think this is cheating or that it somehow makes "Jack Who" less authentic. The sentiment, the feeling, the nostalgia that underpin Carrie's poem are all hers. Students in the class had difficulty understanding the reference to Room 614 until she explained that this was a hospital room. They talked about how she might make this clearer, but Carrie chose to ignore their suggestions.

Jared was one of the students who hadn't done his home-work, but the following morning he slipped this poem onto my desk. He said that Carrie's poem had given him the idea to write about his brother.

Tyler Who

Tyler who is a scrape on the knee
who is a flea to a dog
who is a gnat in your ear
who is annoying
whose hair is molded into spikes
is too cool to say "Sorry"
who tells me I am stupid
but follows in my footsteps
whose blue eyes paint a picture
whose image is everything
can't be second
must be first
who must be the best
a competitor
a football
a basketball
a baseball
who is an athlete
someone who can do it all

who is a champion
will never quit
who will always be there
who will always be my little brother
—*Jared Brunk*

I love this poem. Can't you picture Jared's brother perfectly? Feel the relationship between the two boys and how deeply Jared cares about this kid? I told Jared that he must, must, must show the poem to his mom.

Evaluation

It is at this point and only at this point that we can begin to talk about what makes Sandra Cisneros's "Abuelito Who" a good poem. Too often we teachers ask students if they like a poem or story before we have given them a fair chance to understand it. No one likes something that is incomprehensible. It's so easy for those of us who have taught "Daffodils" or "Dulce et Decorum Est" several dozen times over a decade or two to forget how difficult poems can be to understand on first reading. First comes comprehension, then evaluation.

After multiple readings, discussion, and writing, students were ready to evaluate "Abuelito Who." As they did, they made reference to Cisneros's use of metaphor and the powerful concrete images she employs. They praised her use of repetition, explaining how this gave the poem a rhythm they liked. They applauded Cisneros for managing to write about what could have been an overly sad or sentimental subject without resorting to clichés. They felt she told the truth. I can't help but feel that much of their insight grew out of writing a poem of their own.

Further Resources

■ "Homework for All—in Moderation" by Harris Cooper, *Educational Leadership* 58 (April 2001). One of the findings of this researcher at the University of Missouri–Columbia is that "although common sense dictates that there is a point of diminishing returns, the more homework that high school students do, the higher their achievement levels" (34).

■ Here are two Sandra Cisneros poems from her collection *Loose Woman* that are excellent models for student writing: "The Heart Rounds Up the Usual Suspects" and "Once Again I Prove the Theory of Relativity." The second is perfect for teaching students about similes.

3 A Feast for the Senses

■ ■

As well as being a writer, Sandra Cisneros is an accomplished writing teacher. One technique she shared at a UCLA conference several years ago has become a permanent part of my own teaching repertoire. What Cisneros did was draw a column of childlike images of each of the five senses: an eye, an ear, a nose, a mouth, and a hand. She explained that she often had her students copy these symbols into the margins of pages on which they planned to write in order to remind them to use sensory imagery.

Reading Like a Writer

I immediately saw the potential of this simple graphic not only for creative writers but also for readers. Take, for example, Sandra Cisneros's poem "Good Hotdogs":

> **Good Hotdogs**
> for Kiki
> *Sandra Cisneros*
>
> Fifty cents apiece
> To eat our lunch
> We'd run
> Straight from school
> Instead of home
> Two blocks
> Then the store
> That smelled like steam

You ordered
Because you had the money
Two hotdogs and two pops for here
Everything on the hotdogs
Except pickle lily
Dash those hotdogs
Into buns and splash on
All that good stuff
Yellow mustard and onions
And french fries piled on top all
Rolled up in a piece of wax
Paper for us to hold hot
In our hands
Quarters on the counter
Sit down
Good hotdogs
We'd eat
Fast till there was nothing left
But salt and poppy seeds even
The little burnt tips
Of french fries
We'd eat
You humming
And me swinging my legs

After we read the poem, I asked students to draw a symbol for each of the five senses down the side of the page and draw lines from specific images in the poem that corresponded with the individual senses (see Figure 3.1).

This simple exercise immediately helped students recognize how Cisneros had engaged all their senses. I then invited them to think about what effect this sensory imagery had on their reading of the poem.

JORGE: Reading this poem makes me hungry!

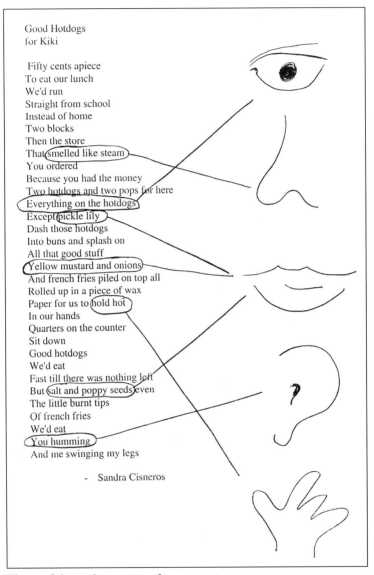

Good Hotdogs
for Kiki

Fifty cents apiece
To eat our lunch
We'd run
Straight from school
Instead of home
Two blocks
Then the store
That smelled like steam
You ordered
Because you had the money
Two hotdogs and two pops for here
Everything on the hotdogs
Except pickle lily
Dash those hotdogs
Into buns and splash on
All that good stuff
Yellow mustard and onions
And french fries piled on top all
Rolled up in a piece of wax
Paper for us to hold hot
In our hands
Quarters on the counter
Sit down
Good hotdogs
We'd eat
Fast till there was nothing left
But salt and poppy seeds even
The little burnt tips
Of french fries
We'd eat
You humming
And me swinging my legs

     - Sandra Cisneros

Figure 3.1 Reading a poem for sensory images.

ANA: Exactly. I mean, it reminded me of walking into a McDonalds when you're starved and you just want to order everything in the place.

MS. JAGO: Show me where. What made you feel that way?

ANA: Well, like that line about the mustard and the onions and the one with the salt and poppy seeds. Yum.

DAVID: French fries!

JORGE: Those hotdogs were calling them. She and her friend run to the store, they "dash them into buns" and "splash on all that good stuff" and then stuff them into their mouths as fast as they can.

ANA: And she's swinging her legs at the end like a kid who's in heaven.

MS. JAGO: You've identified another sense that we didn't draw a symbol for, Ana: our sense of motion. It's sometimes called a kinesthetic sense.

DAVID: What's the symbol for that?

MS. JAGO: I don't know. What do you think?

DAVID: Maybe a bicycle.

JORGE: I'm not drawing any bicycle. She's just happy to be with her friend and happy to be eating hotdogs. I mean, her buddy is humming she's feeling so good.

MS. JAGO: Sounds as though you've put your finger on the tone of this poem.

RACHEL: Happy? Happy isn't a tone, is it?

ANA: Well, maybe not just simple "happy," but I think the poem feels like a good memory Sandra Cisneros had of when she was a kid and simple stuff like hotdogs could make her happy.

I don't think these students could have spoken with such specificity about particular images and the feelings they evoked if the sensory chart hadn't drawn their attention to them so clearly. And their response to Cisneros's imagery brought them naturally to discussion of the poem's tone. I didn't want these students to let go of the poem without noticing one more writer's trick that Cisneros employs. I told the class to follow along as I read the poem aloud and to pay particular attention to what happened at the end of the lines.

RACHEL: It's not how I would have written those lines. I mean, it doesn't make sense to put *wax* at the end of one line and *paper* at the beginning of the next. Or to break up *eat* and *fast*.

MS. JAGO: So why do you think she did?

DAVID: Maybe she wants you to race to the next line without a breath.

JORGE: Yeah, just like she's in a hurry to eat those hotdogs.

MS. JAGO: There's a name for that trick that poets play on us sometimes. It's called "enjambment."

RACHEL: Fancy name.

JORGE: Whatever you want to call it, the whole poem goes by really fast. Short words, short lines. It moves.

Jorge's final comment is an extraordinarily astute description of the tempo of this poem. Cisneros has artfully achieved her purpose without drawing attention to the tools she has employed. As I describe more fully in Chapter 4, drawing attention to mechanism is the teacher's job.

A Conversation with Sandra Cisneros

In 1997 Renée H. Shea conducted an interview with Sandra Cisneros for *The Bookwoman,* the official publication of the Women's National Book Association. Shea taught high school English for many years and is now a professor of English at Bowie State University. She is also a member of NCTE's Comparative and World Literature Committee.

SHEA: In *Woman Hollering Creek* as well as in *Mango Street,* though to a lesser extent, you intersperse Spanish and English. Will that continue in [your new book] *Caramelo?*

CISNEROS: I'm doing it much more conscientiously than ever. In *Mango Street,* I wasn't aware of the Spanish syntax playing a part in that voice until after I wrote it. Now I'm intentionally playing with syntax so that Spanish phrases will gain something humorous by being translated into English. For example, I use part of the Mexican saying "He who is destined to be a tamale" as a chapter title. If you're Mexican, you know that the rest of that saying is "From the heavens fall the cornshucks."

If you are lucky, then everything will fall your way; so if you're destined to be a tamale, even the cornshucks will fall from the sky. It makes no sense in English, but it is a wonderful chapter title! It would lose some of its humor in the original language, but in English I can use it. That's what's so much fun. I can say things like "Uncle Fat Face," which sounds funny, but in Spanish it's not. It's so much a nickname that people don't register what it means anymore.

Those little words and expressions tell you about values. In Spanish you wouldn't even think about the name "Auntie Light Skin," but translating it shows you're putting a value on that light skin. By a word choice, I can let you know that a character is speaking Spanish. Maxine Hong Kingston did that in *The Woman Warrior,* and she criticized Twain: she thought *Huckleberry Finn* would have been a better book if he had used word choice instead of dialect. I think she's right.

SHEA: You [have] said that men and women tell stories in different ways. How do women tell stories?

CISNEROS: I think it depends on culture and class, too. One of the ways for us to tell stories is orally. But now you've put me on the spot because I have to ask, "How did I tell a story in a way that is different from my brothers, people in the same culture?" I'm not concerned with things happening in the way that men are. Some of my male friends want action. When the things that are going on are happening in your heart and head, they say nothing is going on. I'm not preoccupied with where I'm going as much as feeling where the piece is going to go. When I feel it, it's very intuitive. Some of my friends do their stories by outlining, and I do it by feeling, like dancing. One of my closest editors all the way back, a man who is my mentor, says with this new book [*Carmelo*], "You've got to know where it's going!" Well, I haven't a clue where it's going or what it's about. That's how I always write: I just feel something and write from the spots where I feel passionately for that day. If I'm not excited about a story I was working on yesterday and I only have the middle paragraph, I won't write the beginning or end until I feel like it. I'll work on some other things. If I feel sad today because something has happened in my life, then I'm going to use my sadness for my novel. Whatever my passions are—that's what I write. . . .

. . . [W]hen I was in the poetry workshop, I always felt that, as a working-class person, I didn't belong. Rita Dove can tell you I never said "boo," but that doesn't mean I wasn't listening. I was just intimidated by being in a world I felt absolutely inadequate to. But when I look back at the workshop and see who's still writing, the two of us who sat in the back of the room frightened are the ones who are publishing—Joy Harjo and I. We were so terrified that we used to think that maybe we should get a drink before class! When I see Joy now, I say, "You always had the courage to follow your intuition because you knew that was right." I could have gone either way and learned that logical, linear way to write and let go the one I had. I'm really glad she was there for that support and guidance.

SHEA: But didn't it help you to develop as a writer by working with the "masters"?

CISNEROS: It made some people like me sort of resistance fighters. My quiet war was "Okay, this is what you write; let's see what I come up with next week that is just the opposite." They would write about a certain class, so I would take the opposite extreme and take them into my neighborhood. That anger and that distancing accidentally brought me to my place, my center.

My first book of poetry [*My Wicked Wicked Ways*] was too much influenced by the workshop and family leaning over my shoulder. What was wicked for me was that I had no models in my community for being an artist. It was even harder as a daughter to fight for the right of a life of letters—it was a wicked act, to defy everything that was destined for me, what my father thought was best. To live by myself was wicked, and I had to fight my father and older brother just to live alone. . . .

SHEA: After the NPR [National Public Radio] "Book Talk" program on *Mango Street,* you phoned to say that you were disappointed that people focused exclusively on the gender and ethnicity in the work. How do you see class in *Mango Street?*

CISNEROS: Maybe this is a working-class novel because people who are busy working can read one little chapter, then pick it up again! It doesn't intimidate non-book people. My bus-driver cousin told me that he took it to work, and people were reading it out loud and laughing. I love that! It's not a private act but one that can be shared in a public space.

But there were other issues. When I was writing *Mango Street,* I was working with girls who had lives like my neighbors, and I wondered how I had escaped that fate. So I started populating my book with my students and mixing their lives with girlhood memories. The characters became composites and less autobiographical.

An interesting way to look at this book—and no one ever has, but I think it's an important way to read it—is to imagine a writer in her 20s trying to find out what she wants to be. She's trying to find a political consciousness, and she's just discovering that she is "other." The book is about the author discovering her political consciousness, not Esperanza at 12 or 13. I am searching through her for my political ideology. I was too young a writer to make her a medical student or a famous botanist, so I said, "I'll just make her an artist," not realizing that people would think she was me. Then, I realized all along she was a sibyl. She said things that would come true in my life.

That's what I mean when I say that the work is always wiser than the writer. The young writer writing does not have a solution at the time. I didn't know what to do with the part of myself that felt great compassion for my students, and yet here I was teaching them how to write a poem. I felt that it was ridiculous—a little Band-Aid on a hemorrhage. What good was it to teach a girl who has three kids at 17 to write poetry? I thought maybe I should just leave this writing alone and do something else. So, it's me in my 20s searching for some way to change things.

By the time the book ends, Esperanza finds a solution, but I didn't know where it was going to take me as I was writing, nor did I realize that the text itself was going to be my "home in the heart." That's the scary part: there are things in the text that the characters said that came true. The witch woman said, "the home in the heart," and at that time I didn't know what it meant.

SHEA: You've talked about the need for "re-education" in multiculturalism. How does your work contribute to that?

CISNEROS: I want people to recognize themselves in "the other" in my characters. I think that once you see yourself in the other, in that person who is most unlike you, then the story has done its political work. Then we cease to be a "they" or "that" or "those kind," and we become humans. That recognition restores people their humanity, which is the big goal.

I'm in a nice vantage point of being neither Mexican nor completely American. From the middle, I can see the places where the two don't fit. Those interstices are always a rich place to write. When I see that a value does not quite fit in, I know that's what I have to write about.

SHEA: I once heard you describe how you advise your students to pretend they're sitting at the kitchen table in their pajamas. Do you remember that?

Cisneros: Yes, of course. From the years of being socially conditioned, people write in a voice that has a suit on. I get them to write from a true place by having them imagine they are wearing pajamas (or whatever they sleep in). And I like to embellish—so let's say the table is dirty; there are crumbs; the coffee cups are all over. But you're so comfortable with who is sitting across from you that you don't have to clean anything: you can stay just like you are. Who is that one person who could see you just like that, and you wouldn't feel like you had to get up and serve them or make the room tidy?

I think being in a familiar place allows one to get to an authentic speaking voice. Then I say, "Whatever it is you're writing, talk it. Make your hand be the tape recorder; every single syllable, even if it's bad, all those oral digressions are important—talk your piece to that person. If you are speaking to one you trust, your words will come from a true place without fear of mistakes. Then, once it's all done, revise as if your enemy were going to read it!" (2–5)

Writing from a True Place

I often feel the way Sandra Cisneros describes, wondering if teaching kids to write poetry really is what I should be doing. Would it be better simply to focus on skills and make sure they at least know how to spell by the time they leave high school? My middle-class background and sensibilities make most of the guidance I might provide relatively pointless, yet I know that there is a kind of salvation in reading and writing. These students also teach me.

It's a miracle that Brian Menendez is still in school as a senior. Though a brilliant young man, Brian has been shuffled between parents and in many ways has been raised by the gang he runs with. When he offered his poems to me at the beginning of the semester, I was both dazzled by their potential and terrified by the life they describe. It seemed to me that, while providing technical guidance for his poetry writing would be useful, what Brian needed most from me was simply to bear witness.

My Friend's Doctor

My friend is dying
On the way to the hospital
We approach the counter
Exchange words with a nurse
Her nametag reads, "Heather."

My friend's family in a panic
Demanding a stretcher
Heather asks if they have insurance
She explains the law.

We shout and make a scene
Cursing the world as we drive
To County Hospital
A matter of life and death
Internal bleeding

Your life in their hands
And they hand it back

> Because you can't pay the bill
> We drive
> I wipe tears
> from my friend's mother's face.
>
> At County my friend's doctor
> Tells us he was five minutes late.
> —*Brian Menendez*

In another poem, Brian describes young people "turning to drugs / because they can't turn / to anyone else." The more I read his work, the more I am convinced that he is truly writing from what Cisneros calls "a true place." There is no glorification of what Brian is living through in these poems but rather a lament that things cannot be otherwise. He writes of "Taking those into my heart who are poor / wanting to free the needy like Schindler / Living in a system that manipulates my adolescent nation / worse than Hitler." He describes his neighborhood as "neighborhood concentration camps" where he has been "sentenced to death" (remember, this is sunny Santa Monica where movie stars live, too).

I don't know if writing can save Brian's life. He is a natural leader and as a result often finds himself on the front line of any trouble. I am convinced that the world would be a better place for all if we could find more room for voices like Brian's to be heard.

Further Resources

■ For another interview with Sandra Cisneros, this one by Reed Dasenbrock, go to http://acunix.wheatonma.edu/rpearce/MultiC_Web/Authors/Sandra_Cisneros/body_sandra_cisneros.html. In it, Cisneros discusses the bilingual aspects of her writing.

■ The Sandra Cisneros Teacher Resource File at http://falcon.jmu. edu/~ramseyil/cisneros.htm includes biography, bibliography, book reviews, lesson plans, and ERIC resources.

4 Teaching Literary Terminology in Context

■ ■

In *Literature as Exploration,* Louise Rosenblatt asserted, "The problem that the teacher faces first of all, then, is the creation of a situation favorable to a vital experience of literature. Unfortunately, many of the practices and much of the tone of literature teaching have precisely the opposite effect" (61). Remembering how we had been taught literature in high school, with heavy emphasis on form and background over any kind of authentic reader response, many of us embraced Rosenblatt's theories with open arms. We stopped teaching students about authors' lives and about how the work fit into the literary canon and instead focused on eliciting from students authentic reader responses. We also banished any reference to literary terminology. In retrospect, I think this was a mistake. I also don't think for a minute that this was what Rosenblatt intended.

The language of literature helps readers express what they see in what they read. Terms such as "personification," "alliteration," and "metaphor" give us words to describe how a particular poem or passage affects us. Banishing these words from our classroom vocabulary makes students less, not more, articulate about literature.

While the study of a poem should never be an exercise in identification—find the simile, state the theme, explain the allusion: a game of literary trivial pursuit—we need to teach students the vocabulary of literature study. It is important to show them how literary terms describe the tools writers use to convey meaning. I try to demonstrate how understanding literary terminology can help us unpack a poem's meaning. Take Sandra Cisneros's "Peaches—Six in a Tin Bowl, Sarajevo," for example:

Peaches—Six in a Tin Bowl, Sarajevo
Sandra Cisneros

If peaches had arms
surely they would hold one another
in their peach sleep.

And if peaches had feet
it is sure they would
nudge one another
with their soft peachy feet.

And if peaches could
they would sleep
with their dimpled head
on the other's
each to each.

Like you and me.

And sleep and sleep.

Prereading

When students arrive for class, the first thing they see on the board is a definition of personification:

Personification: a figure of speech in which abstract ideas, in-animate objects, or animals are given human characteristics.

I ask students to copy this definition into their notebooks. Too often teachers underestimate the power of copying. When we hand students something like this definition of personification on a neatly typed handout, most teenagers feel that they don't need to read it. Why bother? They know they have it somewhere (have it, that is, until they walk out the door and lose it to the wind, or to the jumble that is their backpack, or for use as a paper airplane). Copying the words from the board is one baby step toward making the term their own. This two-minute activity also helps bring the group to order.

Reading the Poem

I then hand out copies of "Peaches—Six in a Tin Bowl, Sarajevo" and read it aloud. At this point, it is too early to elicit student responses. Even in an obedient class that has seemingly paid attention to my reading, most students' minds are still elsewhere. If I were to begin our class discussion at this point, the same two or three students who always respond would raise their hands, and a minidiscussion between me and these predictable few would ensue. It would likely run out of steam in a few minutes, and I would fill in the rest of the time allotted to this lesson doing all the talking myself.

Instead, I ask students to read the poem again to themselves, marking places where they have questions, underlining phrases they like, annotating passages that remind them of something or someone. A few students take this as an invitation to illustrate the text. When I see that most have finished, I have students exchange their annotated poem with a partner and ask them to read the poem through again and then comment on their classmate's comments, engaging in a kind of silent discussion of the poem.

When students get their own papers back, there is almost always a demand for me to referee certain readings. "Mrs. Jago, Tony says _____ but I think _____. Who's right?" This is the place where I can throw open the discussion by inviting their now considered reader responses.

Teaching Personification

If during our discussion no one makes the connection between the poem and the definition of personification before them on the board, I draw students' attention once again to the term and ask what they think about the way Cisneros gave peaches the characteristics of human beings:

> What are these peaches doing with their arms and feet?
> How did this make you feel?
> What do you think Cisneros is trying to say here?
> How do you imagine she got the idea for doing this?

I ask students to write for five minutes below their copied definition about Cisneros's use of personification in "Peaches—Six in a Tin Bowl, Sarajevo." Molly Meers wrote:

> Personification in "Peaches"
> At first I thought it was kind of gross. Picturing peaches hugging made me think of squashed fruit, bruised and all mushy. But then when I reread the poem I thought she was probably looking at a bowl of peaches and thinking about somebody she loved. Maybe somebody she couldn't touch right now but wanted to. Maybe remembering a time when their toes could touch when they used to sleep together like soft peaches in a bowl.

Suddenly "personification" was no longer a fussy term that only

English teachers use, but rather a way to describe how poets find fresh ways to talk about love and longing.

The Use and Misuse of Background Information

When Molly read her quickwrite to the class, I was faced with a dilemma. There were things I knew about Sandra Cisneros and Sarajevo that might deepen students' understanding of the poem. On the other hand, this information could also undermine their readings and make students feel that their interpretations were somehow inferior to my "informed" interpretation.

Here's what I knew: In 1993 a friend of Sandra Cisneros's from Sarajevo wrote her a letter describing conditions in the city during the Bosnian conflict. Jasna described how the ancient city of Sarajevo had been heavily bombed and its people forced to live in terrible conditions amidst the rubble. Cisneros was so moved by Jasna's letter that she sent it to every major newspaper in the United States. You can find a copy in the *New York Times* archives (April 9, 1993, p. A12). A few days later the *New York Times* published an article by Cisneros protesting conditions in Sarajevo and calling on the government to intervene. In "Who Wants Stories Now," Cisneros wrote, "A woman is there. . . . She's in that city, that country, that region, that mouth of hell, that house on fire. . . . I hear that somebody. And I know that somebody. And I don't know what to do. I don't know what to do" (17).

Louise Rosenblatt has written that "all such facts are expendable unless they demonstrably help to clarify or enrich individual experiences of specific novels, poems, or plays. The notion of 'background information' often masks much that is irrelevant and distracting" (27). In the end, I chose to share what I knew with students, deciding that this information about Jasna and Sarajevo was relevant to their reading of the poem. This is a tricky issue, though, and in other circumstances I might choose otherwise.

Necessary Literary Terminology

The following literary terms enrich classroom conversations about literature. Mastering this vocabulary has also helped to make the transition to Advanced Placement courses and college English classes much less stressful for students. You won't need to quiz students on these definitions if you use the terms regularly.

> **Alliteration:** The repetition of initial consonant sounds, as in "pretty purple petunias" in the vignette "A House of My Own" from *The House on Mango Street*. Alliteration draws our attention to something. It can also be a powerful tool for memory.

> **Archetype:** A prototype on which characters, images, stories, or themes are modeled. The character Elenita, who reads tarot cards for Esperanza and tells her future, is modeled after the witch/wise woman archetype. In the vignette "The Three Sisters," the three women who "did not seem to be related to anything but the moon" (103) are contemporary representatives of the archetypal three Fates. They tell Esperanza, "When you leave you must remember to come back for the others. A circle, understand? You will always be Esperanza. You will always be Mango Street" (105).

> **Connotation:** The suggestion or implication of a word or expression. Though *house* and *home* have the same denotation of "a place of shelter," the two words have very different connotations. You might, for example, want to ask students why

Esperanza doesn't consider the house on Mango Street her real home. In the vignette "No Speak English," Cisneros writes, "Home. Home. Home is a house in a photograph" (77).

Diction: A writer's word choice. See discussion of Cisneros's simple, childlike diction in "Good Hotdogs" in Chapter 3. Her choice of "pickle lily" and "yellow mustard and onions" rather than "condiments" helps create the poem's tone.

Figurative language: Language used in suggestive rather than literal ways. Figurative language in poetry includes simile, metaphor, and personification. For example, "Abuelito who throws coins like rain."

Hyperbole: Intentional overstatement. In the vignette "And Some More" from *The House on Mango Street,* Nenny insists that there are "a million zillion" (35) kinds of snow. Overstatement is often used for humor, as in Voltaire's *Candide.*

Imagery: Verbal pictures or other sensory detail. The vignette "Hairs" from *The House on Mango Street* is rich in sensory imagery:

> But my mother's hair, my mother's hair, like little rosettes, like little candy circles all curly and pretty because she pinned it in pincurls all day, sweet to put your nose into when she is holding you, holding you and you feel safe, is the warm smell of bread before you bake it, is the smell when she makes room for you on her side of the bed still warm with her skin, and you sleep near her, the rain outside falling and Papa snoring. The snoring, the rain, and Mama's hair that smells like bread. (6–7)

Irony: The tension that arises from the discrepancy either between what one says and what one means (verbal irony) or between what a character believes and what a reader knows (dramatic irony). **Sarcasm** is conspicuously bitter and mocking irony. One of the most famous instances of sarcasm occurs in Shakespeare's *Julius Caesar* when Mark Antony calls Brutus an "honorable man."

Metaphor: A figure of speech that makes a direct comparison without the use of the words *like* or *as*; for example, in "Abuelito Who": "who is dough and feathers/ who is a watch and glass of water." We often employ metaphors in everyday speech such as when we describe a newborn baby as "a little doll," or when we say, "Peter is a road hog."

Narrative poem: The telling of a story in verse with a focus on a single incident, as in "Good Hotdogs."

Onomatopoeia: The use of words whose sound implies their meaning. Poets employ onomatopoeia in an attempt to represent a thing or action by a word that imitates the sound associated with it; for example: *zoom, crash, ding-dong, whiz.* Emily Dickinson imitated the droning of a fly in the line "uncertain stumbling Buzz" through the combination of nasal (*n, m, ng*) and sibilant (*c, s*) sounds.

Personificaton: A figure of speech in which abstract ideas, inanimate objects, or animals are given human characteristics. See discussion of "Peaches—Six in a Tin Bowl, Sarajevo" in this chapter.

Prose poem: A form of prose characterized by rhythmic patterns and figurative language similar to that of poetry. Many of the vignettes in *The House on Mango Street* can be considered prose poems. "Darius & the Clouds" is a perfect example.

Refrain: A sentence or phrase of one line or more repeated in a poem, often at the end of a stanza or between stanzas. A refrain whose words change slightly with each recurrence is called an **incremental refrain.** Another variation is the **internal refrain,** which appears within a stanza, most often in a position that remains fixed throughout the poem. Students know many popular songs that employ refrains.

Rhyme: Repetition of sound in accented syllables that appear in similar positions within lines of poetry. The best rhymes surprise a reader. One of the most characteristic features of "bad" poetry is rhyme for the sake of rhyme. Alexander Pope describes what this sounds like:

> Where'er you find "the cooling western breeze,"
> In the next line it "whispers through the trees";
> If crystal streams "with pleasing murmurs creep,"
> The reader's threatened (not in vain) with "sleep"

Rhythm: The regular recurrence and speed of sound and stresses in a poem or work of prose. Writers use rhythm to intensify the meaning of words, slowing it when the effect is reflective (as in "Abuelito Who") and hastening it to portray excitement (for example, when the girls are running to the store in "Good Hotdogs").

Simile: A figure of speech that makes a comparison between two objects using the word *like* or *as.* In the vignette "Laughter" from *The House on Mango Street,* the narrator says that her and her sister Nenny's laughter is "like a pile of dishes breaking" (17). In the short story "One Holy Night" in *Woman Hollering Creek,* Cisneros writes,

> Rachel says that love is like a big black piano being pushed off the top of a three-story building and you're waiting on the bottom to catch it. But Lourdes says it's not that way at all. It's like a top, like all the colors in the world are spinning so fast they're not colors anymore and all that's left is a white hum. (35)

Writers often use similes for concepts such as love that are difficult to describe.

Tone: The attitude expressed by the style and overall presentation of a piece of writing, and reflected mainly through syntax and diction. See the discussion of the mood and tone of "Good Hotdogs" in Chapter 3.

Further Resources

■ An excellent anthology of poetry that provides cross-references for poems and literary terms is *Poetry in Six Dimensions, 20th Century Voices,* edited by Carol Clark and Norma Fifer (Cambridge, MA: Educators Publishing Service, 2000).

■ The National Council of Teachers of English has published a book by a former Australian high school teacher, Brian Moon, called *Literary Terms: A Practical Glossary* (Urbana, IL: NCTE, 1999).

The volume offers ideas about how to make the shift from teaching terms for the sake of identification to teaching literary concepts as tools for thoughtful reading. Instead of viewing literature as a body of objective knowledge to be mastered, Moon considers it a field of social practice within which readers and writers act. In the chapter on imagery, for example, Moon quotes Samuel Taylor Coleridge from *The Rime of the Ancient Mariner:* "Day after day, day after day, / We stuck, nor breath nor motion; / As idle as a painted ship upon a painted ocean." The questions that follow do not ask students to identify the imagery but instead invite them to think about whether the mental pictures that Coleridge's words create have been generated by the words themselves or by a combination of these words and the reader's own experiences and memories. Moon then asks whether one can ever be sure that the images one "sees" are the same as those another reader sees. This is the kind of teaching that helps students become thoughtful readers. It also avoids the dissection model of literary analysis. Each chapter in *Literary Terms* offers an opening problem that brings the concept into focus, followed by a brief theoretical discussion. Moon then provides a sample student activity through which students can apply the concept to a piece of literature, and he closes with a working definition of the term. It is a useful model for any teacher, novice or expert.

■ A resource I could not do without on my shelves is *Benét's Reader's Encyclopedia* (edited by Bruce Murphy, 4th edition, New York: HarperCollins, 1996).

5 The House That Everybody Knows

The House on Mango Street is a collection of forty-four interwoven stories describing the life of Esperanza, a young girl coming of age in a Latino barrio. Along with painting a vivid portrait of Esperanza's life, the book explores the cultural forces that pull Esperanza in opposite directions. Should she follow her dreams out of the neighborhood or remain within the circle of her family and friends? Is it possible to do both? Though populated by a large cast of characters who lack power—politically, socially, sexually, and economically—Esperanza's story is full of hope.

One of the most extraordinary qualities of this book is how it can be enjoyed by readers of almost any age. Even very young children will respond to the sensory imagery of the vignette "Hairs," and in fact that particular story from *The House on Mango Street* has been published as a picture book. For many twelve- to fourteen-year-old readers, the book will be a mirror in which they find reflected their own feelings and experiences. For older readers, the book offers a window through which to view the race-class-gender paradigm that characterizes the Latino experience in the United States. It is a sturdy little volume that bears rereading and invites multiple interpretive stances.

Cisneros has said that the character sketches and vignettes add up "to tell one big story, each story contributing to the whole—like beads in a necklace."

Where to Begin

At my high school, *The House on Mango Street* is a core text in the ninth-grade curriculum. In an ideal world, I would hand out copies of *The House on Mango Street* and ask students to read the book in a single sitting without any introductory information or a single preparatory activity. There is a power to the whole that can sometimes get lost when the text is parceled out over a two- to four-week teaching unit. At the same time, I have been in the classroom too many years to think that a typical group of ninth graders would be likely to complete my ideal Day One assignment. Only a few have the reading stamina necessary to open up a text and not put it down for the next hour or two until it's done.

Instead, we begin with the first vignette, "The House on Mango Street." I read the piece aloud to help students hear the speaker's voice. It is important to make students aware that any reading like this is in fact an interpretation of the text. When students are further along in the book, an interesting assignment is to have them prepare an oral reading of one of the vignettes and discuss how these readings reflect the various readers' interpretations of Cisneros's story.

The opening vignette invites all kinds of discussion about houses and homes. I always like to include a two-minute lesson on connotation and denotation, pointing out how though *house* and *home* have similar dictionary definitions (denotations), their connotations are very different. This simple explanation often takes our conversation to a new depth.

Ms. Jago: So what does the difference between *house* and *home* have to do with this story?

Tracey: Well, for one thing this small red house is just a building where the girl lives. She doesn't want it to be her home.

Ms. Jago: Why not?

Maria: Because she wants the house that will be her real home to be like a house on TV and have a big back yard, not all nasty and crumbling like this one.

Tracey: Yeah, besides, the story is called "The House on Mango Street," not "The Home on Mango Street." The girl keeps talking about someday living in a "real house." I agree with Maria. That real house would be her home.

Oscar: But it's kind of sad because she's gotta live where she's gotta live. If you're always dreaming about big houses with swimming pools, well, that's dumb because you're always going to be unhappy with where you are.

Tracey: I guess, but if she didn't dream of something besides this crummy house, maybe she'd be even more unhappy.

Oscar and Tracey have anticipated the bittersweet tone of Cisneros's book. What an excellent way to begin!

Questioning the Author

I had been working on a technique for developing discussion questions that borrowed from Isabel Beck and colleagues' questioning-the-author research. Instead of "gotcha" questions that simply assess student comprehension after reading, Beck's "queries" assist students as they grapple with text in order to construct meaning.

I asked students to consider the order of the first four vignettes. Why might Cisneros have chosen to have the narrator tell us about her house, her family's hair, and the children in her neighborhood before telling us about her name? Questions like this help students realize that authors make conscious decisions about such things. Many teenagers simply assume that books are written almost as if by magic—as if the story has been told the only way it could have been told. I want to help them see how authors must make many choices as they construct their stories, and that part of our job as good readers is to think about why they might have chosen one way rather than another.

Some questions that have helped me get kids thinking about Cisneros's choices include:

- Why do you think Cisneros decided to tell this story from the point of view of the young girl Esperanza? How old do you think she is? How does the childlike quality of her voice affect you? What would change if the narrator were a boy?

- How does Cisneros show you what Esperanza's neighborhood and family are like? Find concrete descriptive details in these four vignettes that offer the reader information about the book's setting.

- What effect does breaking the story up into small pieces have on you? Are you annoyed? Distracted? Engaged? Confused? Charmed? All of the above? Do you think it is cheating for an author not to write transitions between these separate pieces?

- How would you describe Cisneros's diction? How does her choice of words create a mood or tone for the book? Find a paragraph that provides a good example of diction contributing to tone.

I then offered students a list of "queries" that we would use throughout our reading of *The House on Mango Street*. We talked about how these questions encourage a different kind of discussion from that generated when I ask them, "Where did the narrator live before she moved to the house on Mango Street?" or "Who are the members of Esperanza's family?" We posted this list of queries on the bulletin board and used them whenever the momentum of our conversation about the book flagged.

- What is the author trying to say here?
- What is the author's message?
- What does the author mean when she says _____?
- How does this story connect with what you know about houses, or neighborhoods, or names?
- Has the story changed your thinking about these things in any way? Explain why or why not.

Courtney Cazden has said, "It is easy to imagine talk in which ideas are explored rather than answers to teachers' test questions provided and evaluated. . . . Easy to imagine, but not easy to do" (112). I am constantly looking for ways to encourage authentic classroom discussion, the kind in which students actually talk about the things in a text that they care about rather than the things I have determined they should care about. It's a delicate balance to strike.

Thinking Out Loud

Despite all my best efforts at engagement, some students remained resistant to reading *The House on Mango Street*. Though their eyes were passing over the lines of text, they seemed to be taking in little and barely responding. Taking a cue from my elementary school colleagues, I tried the strategy of "think-alouds" to demonstrate for these readers what it is that I do in my head as I read. I chose the vignette "Gil's Furniture Bought & Sold" and read it aloud, including commentary and questions that represented my internal dialogue.

In the following paragraph, Cisneros's words appear in normal typeface, and my commentary is in italics. Whenever you model a think-aloud for students, it is important to include an example of connecting the text to your own experience, as well as an example of either readjusting or confirming an early assumption.

> There is a junk store. An old man owns it. *I can just picture this. The guy is probably bent over and dusty.* We bought a used refrigerator from him once, and Carlos sold a box of magazines for a dollar. *Strange place if the guy deals in both used refrigerators and old magazines. It's probably a mess.* The store is small with just a dirty window for light. *Kinda spooky.* He doesn't turn the lights on unless you got money to buy things with, so in the dark we look and see all kinds of things, me and Nenny. *Yeh, just like I thought! Maybe these kids see things that aren't really there.* Tables with their feet upside-down and rows and rows of refrigerators with round corners *I remember those from when I was a kid in Chicago* and couches that spin dust in the air when you punch them *Yep, just like I thought—dusty* and a hundred T.V.'s that don't work probably. Everything is on top of everything so the whole store has skinny aisles *funny way to describe aisles, I usually only think of people as skinny* to walk through. You can get lost easy. *Lost in your imagination, too.* (19)

I then ask students to work with a partner doing the same thing out loud for the rest of the story, alternating paragraphs. We then talk about what they noticed happening as they read in this manner. It begins to dawn on students that "reading" really means "thinking." For some this is an epiphany.

Educational researchers often recommend that teachers tape these students' readings, but I'll bet none of them meets 150 students a day or has ever considered how many hours of listening this would entail. One of the things I like best about this think-aloud strategy is that it is productive for students without being labor intensive for me. Apart from preparing the think-aloud model paragraph, there are no other handouts to copy before the lesson or student papers to read after the lesson. Most good teachers can't work any harder. We need to learn to work smarter.

Mango Street as Inspiration for Personal Writing

Sandra Cisneros's writing almost cries out to be used as a model for student writing. The vignettes from the beginning and near the end of the book, "The House on Mango Street" and "A House of My Own," can be used to inspire students to write about their homes and the homes they would like to live in. Students should use language that both tells the reader what the houses look like and reveals what they feel about these places.

The vignette "My Name" is perfect for helping students get to know one another. Writing about their own names inevitably causes young people to reveal things about their own cultural heritage and background. Sharing these writings with their classmates helps to create community within the classroom.

Eleazar

In a different language my name means "God help." In English it means one big headache to the teacher who reads it out loud. The problem got so bad that my science teacher started to call me "Hey, you in the back." Some of my friends pronounce it wrong (actually most of my friends). The origin of this name came from some guy in the Bible. I changed the spelling later because I liked this other guy in the Bible more. Then I finally couldn't make up my mind so I cross-breeded them and ended up with Eleazar. Some of my parents' friends call me by a formal name with a really funny sounding pronunciation, kind of like saying my name with their tongue at the back of their mouths. Overall, I think it suits my personality.

Amanda

"To be loved." That's what my name means. I can't say whether it holds true. I don't like to judge myself like that. However my feeling tells me that in order to be loved you must give love, like the magic mush pot. I know I shovel out the mush. It even says so in my character as a Libra. I try and sometimes don't try but still see the beauty in things that I'm acquainted with. When I was younger I wanted to change my name. Perhaps it was because I so desperately wanted to be anyone else but myself. I've realized within the past couple of years that changing my name wouldn't change me except maybe give me another mask to hide behind.

Farnaz

My name lies in my past in ancient Persia, in the way of life of an ancient poet, Chayam, who wrote about love and wine, about eternity, about death, always about wine. My name is the name of a woman in my past, mystic, warm, gracious, offering wine to strangers passing by and always spilling some into the dust of the earth for those who the earth has received into itself. My name is Farnaz. It describes a way of life: rough, ancient. It persists today and will always be in places where there is no room for time to pass, no room for minutes, no room for stress, anxiety, or pain. Only love. And for the day by day.

Jin Sun

It was a clear Wednesday night. It was very humid and the roads were jammed pack with cars. It was quite unusual for such a heavy traffic at that hour, but not that week. It was the week of Explore '74. It was where ministers taught the word of the Lord to great crowds that gathered in the auditorium. One such minister was patiently waiting in his car for the traffic to die down. It was a great crowd tonight. They were eager and attentive. He smiled to himself thinking of the service. He then thought about his wife and wondered how she was doing. He was worried about how the pregnancy was affecting her. She was weak and their second child came out premature. The first one died within a few hours and the minister wondered about this one. Thinking about the baby made him smile again. It was going to be a boy and they had a name picked out and everything. He wouldn't have to worry about his family name being carried out any more. With these thoughts, he went home.

Early the next day, his wife went into labor. He dropped her off at the hospital and went to get his mother. She was excited about it being a boy also. When the minister arrived he found out that the baby was already delivered. He eagerly ran to where his wife was and look! It was a beautiful baby girl! His mother was immensely disappointed, but the minister couldn't be happier. She was as healthy as they came and his wife was well. The only problem was the name.

As the minister pondered over it awhile, he came up with something wonderful. He decided to name her Jin Sun. Jin meaning truth and Sun meaning sharing. For she was born when he was spreading the word. She must be called Jin Sun . . . distributing the truth. Two hours after Jin Sun was born, there was a great commotion. At first, her parents thought that it was the Korean Independence Day celebration, but after a few minutes they found out what it was. The first lady of Korea was assassinated. For every life gone, a new one is born.

My favorite Cisneros vignette to use as inspiration for personal writing is "Hairs." As I was going though my files in preparation for writing this book, I came on a short piece that I had written with the class and published in our class anthology. The James I describe in my vignette is now heading off to college.

James's Hair
Reaching down to kiss you good-bye, the backpack holding
your lunch larger than your back, I suddenly recoil.
"Eeugggghhh! You didn't wash your hair last night!"
Fresh boy-stink rises from your head. The day-old sweat
seems to talk to me of soccer games won and lost, panting
dreams, even a trip to the nurse's office. I could learn about
you, about your secret child life if I listened to your hair. I
might penetrate our, "What-did-you-do-in-school-today? Oh-
nothing" conversations.
But I'm too busy playing mom, upholder of family hygiene.
—*Carol Jago, 1989*

Sandra Cisneros's story "Hairs" is a tiny piece, two short paragraphs that reveal much about Esperanza's family and family relationships. I don't belabor an analysis of the vignette but instead
simply invite students to do as Cisneros has done—use sensory
imagery and metaphors to write about hair. Some students choose
to write about their own hair, others about family members' hair.
In my experience, students do not so much imitate Cisneros's
style as follow her intent, using hair as a vehicle for writing about
something that matters to them.

The Long and Short of It
My hair covers one eye and as a result cannot be trained by
sprays or gels to stay in place for very long. It has the texture of
nine-grain sandpaper and was jet black when I was younger. It
has since lost its sheen and has been reduced to a non-lustrous
tuft of thin brittle strands, a fact my mother continually nags
about and has attributed to the extensive use of chemicals to
tame it.
I don't think anyone really appreciates having to look at my
tuft. People constantly tell me to cut it because they say it makes
me look effeminate. I like it because the conformist eyes of the

Asian establishment despise it and think it represents an Asian stereotype gone awry.

—*Koki Ichiroku*

Her Hair Tells a Story

My mom's hair is intriguing because it's forbidden, like something you want to possess because you're not allowed to have it. Her hair sometimes looks like Medusa's, yet instead of turning you into stone, she'll make you feel good about yourself. She doesn't mind what it looks like. Without a care in the world, she just washes it and lets it go. Her hair has seen many perms, "The Flip," "The Beehive," and now she tries for the Cybill Shepherd look which she has been unsuccessful with, because her hair can't be anything but what it is. It runs free, like wild horses along the ocean.

My mom's hair is wired like she stuck her finger in an electrical socket. Some gray and some brown; they go in all directions, like children the minute summer vacation begins. Her hair stands out among the others. They look out over her and guide her way through chaos, like tentacles feeling their way through the world to see if it's safe.

I remember one day I came home from Sunday school, she had dyed her hair black. My eyes nearly jumped out of my head, and the peach fuzz on the back of my neck stood on end. That wasn't my mother, it was Connie Chung! Now it is back to normal, normal for her, that is.

If I were small enough I would curl up in it and make it my home, all soft and white. There is so much of it, I could sleep in a different part each night. One thing for sure, if you lose her in a crowd you can always find her. In the mall, the park, or in a crowd of millions, you just look for my mother's zany gray hair and you'll find her, you'll see.

—*Becky Neiman*

Given students who write such honest, compelling narratives, it is easy to see why I love teaching. One concern I have is that in some states (my own included) personal writing is in danger of being pushed out of the curriculum in favor of analytical and persuasive forms. One of the best arguments I know of for continuing to include personal writing in any course of study was put forth by T. S. Eliot:

> We shall not cease from exploration
> And the end of all our exploring
> Will be to arrive where we started
> And know the place for the first time.
> "Little Gidding," *Four Quartets*

In order to write persuasively and analytically, students must not only know the world, but they must also know themselves.

Further Resources

Extensive study guides and detailed outlines for teaching *The House on Mango Street* are readily available, many of them on the Web.

- *The House on Mango Street,* "A Three Week Unit Plan" by Paul E. Turtola can be found at http://www.ncte.org/books/42311/resources/turtola.shtml. The site includes supplementary readings about Cisneros's purple house in San Antonio and critical reviews about her receipt of a MacArthur genius grant that students will find interesting.

- A Vintage Books Teachers Guide to *The House on Mango Street* is available at http://www.randomhouse.com/acmart/houmantg.html. The guide contains notes for teachers, as well as a long list of discussion questions.

- Jane Schaffer Publications offers a study guide for teaching *The House on Mango Street* at http://www.curriculumguides.com/.

6 Taking a Critical Stance

Teachers regularly ask students to assume a critical stance. Often, analytical essays are the principle tool we use to judge students' ability to scrutinize literature. What we rarely do is offer students samples of professional literary criticism. I believe that reading what others have said about a writer's work can help students refine their own thinking. The following excerpts from critical essays on Sandra Cisneros can provide fodder for further discussion as well as for students' own essays.

Readings

Janet Sarbanes

This excerpt from Janet Sarbanes's essay evaluates *The House on Mango Street* as a Chicana coming of age story.

> Critics have identified the novel as an example of the growing up story, or *bildungsroman,* which forms a general theme of Chicano and Chicana literature. But Cisneros's text differs from the traditional Chicano bildungsroman, in which the boy becomes a man by first acquiring self-sufficiency and then assuming his rightful place as a leader in the community. It also differs from the traditional Chicana bildungsroman, in which the girl must give up her freedom and sense of individuality in order to join the community as

a wife and mother. The goal of Esperanza, this novel's protagonist and narrator, is to fashion an identity for herself which allows her to control her own destiny and at the same time maintain a strong connection to her community. . . .

By making the narrator of her novel a preadolescent girl, Cisneros represents Mango Street from the point of view of someone who is not yet placed, not yet put into position. Esperanza's is a voice that can question, a voice of hope, a voice of transition. She is not inside the house looking out, like many of the other girls and women, nor is she outside the community looking in with strange eyes, like the nuns. Often she is out in the street, looking in at the other women —observing, analyzing, evaluating their situation. . . .

While Esperanza may not accept the house on Mango Street as her home—that is to say, while she may refuse to accept the self that is handed to her—she does ultimately accept Mango Street as part of herself.

Source: Janet Sarbanes, 1997. Essay in *Novels for Students. Volume 2: Presenting Analysis, Context and Criticism on Commonly Studied Novels,* edited by Diane Telgen, Kevin Hile, Marie Rose Napierkowski, and Sheryl Ciccarelli. Detroit: Gale Research. 123–26.

▪ ▪ ▪ ▪ ▪ ▪ ▪ ▪ ▪ ▪ ▪ ▪ ▪ ▪ ▪ ▪

Thomas Matchie

Thomas Matchie compares *The House on Mango Street* with *Huckleberry Finn* and *The Catcher in the Rye.*

In 1963 in a collection of articles entitled *Salinger,* Edgar Branch has a piece in which he explores the literary continuity between Mark Twain's *The Adventures of Huckleberry*

Finn and J. D. Salinger's *Catcher in the Rye.* Branch claims that, though these two books represent different times in American history, the characters, the narrative patterns and styles, and the language are strikingly similar, so that what Salinger picks up, according to Branch, is an archetypal continuity which is cultural as well as literary. I would like to suggest a third link in this chain that belongs to our own time, and that is Sandra Cisneros's *The House on Mango Street.* Published in 1989, this novella is about an adolescent, though this time a girl who uses, not the Mississippi or Manhattan Island, but a house in Chicago to examine her society and the cultural shibboleths that weigh on her as a young Chicana woman. . . .

Cisneros, like Twain and Salinger, seems to enter the narrative to help define its ultimate meaning. Unlike the boys' quests, however, this novel is a collection of genres—essays, short stories, poems—put together in one way to show Esperanza's growth, but in another to imitate the part-by-part building of an edifice. Indeed, the house on Mango Street does not just refer to the place Esperanza is trying to leave, but to the novel itself as "a house" which Esperanza as character and Cisneros as author have built together. Huck may go out to the territory, rejecting civilization, and Holden may tell his story to gain the strength to return, but Esperanza through her writing has in fact redesigned society itself through a mythical house of her own.

Source: Thomas Matchie, 1995. "Literary Continuity in Sandra Cisneros's *The House on Mango Stree.*" *The Midwest Quarterly* 37 (Autumn): 67–69.

Rick Martinez

This excerpt is taken from a Hispanic Link News Service article by Rick Martinez called "Geniuses Can Come in Many Colors."

Only 24 hours after writer Sandra Cisneros was honored with one of the nation's most prestigious awards, the tribute was dismissed by a New York art critic who sniffed that the John D. and Catherine T. MacArthur Foundation was simply being politically correct. . . . In a National Public Radio commentary, critic Edward Lisson took issue with this year's selections, implying that Anglo males were overlooked. . . .

Lisson's commentary does, in a large sense, illustrate the growing wave of passive-aggressive anger being directed at Hispanics and other groups on many levels. Whether the topic is diversity in the work place, affirmative action, or the John D. and Catherine T. MacArthur genius awards, ethnics of color and women who achieve some level of success are all too often measured against an imaginary white male who must have been passed over for this non-white male person to have succeeded. . . .

As Cisneros and her contemporaries take the Hispanic experience to the next level, there are those in the establishment who figure she must be the honoree in a beauty contest of political correctness, no doubt displacing much more deserving non-ethnic males who happen not to be the flavor of the day.

Source: Rick Martinez, 1995. "Geniuses Can Come in Many Colors." *Houston Chronicle* (November 12): F1.

▪ ▪ ▪ ▪ ▪ ▪ ▪ ▪ ▪ ▪ ▪ ▪ ▪ ▪ ▪ ▪ ▪

Dianne Klein

In an essay for *English Journal,* Dianne Klein explores Esperanza's coming of age as a political act. The entire article is reprinted here.

Coming of Age in Novels by
Rudolfo Anaya and Sandra Cisneros

At birth, each person begins a search to know the world and others, to answer the age-old question, "Who am I?" This search for knowledge, for truth, and for personal identity is written about in autobiographies and in bildungsroman fiction. For years, though, the canon of United States literature has included predominantly the coming-of-age stories of white, heterosexual males. Where are the stories of the others—the women, the African Americans, the Asian Americans, the Hispanics, the gay males and lesbians? What differences and similarities would we find in their bildungsromans? Many writers, silenced before, are now finding the strengths, the voices, and the market for publication to tell their stories.

Chicano/a writers, like African Americans, Asian Americans, and others, are being heard; in autobiography and in fiction, they are telling their coming-of-age stories. *Bless Me, Ultima* by Rudolfo Anaya (1972) and *The House on Mango Street* by Sandra Cisneros (1989) are two such Chicano/a works of fiction. In these texts, Anaya and Cisneros show the forces—social and cultural—that shape and define their characters. These two novels, separated by about a generation, one about the male experience, one about the female; one rural, one urban; one mythopoetic and one dialectic, both show the struggle of the Chicano/a people to find identities that are true to themselves as individuals and artists but that do not betray their culture and their people.

This is no mean feat, considering that Anglos did not teach them to value their cultural heritage and experiences, that they were shown no Chicano/a role models, that, in fact, they were often discouraged from writing. The struggle to overcome these barriers may, of course, be different for different Chicano/a writers, but for these two, there are common threads. Both make similar comments about their roots. Anaya says that Chicano/a writers

> came from poor families . . . but we were rich with love and culture and a sense of sharing and imagination. We had to face a school system that very often told us we couldn't write. It did not teach us our own works and we had nothing to emulate. (Bruce-Novoa 1980, 198)

Cisneros says that as a writer growing up without models of Chicano/a literature, she felt impoverished with nothing of personal merit to say.

> As a poor person growing up in a society where the class norm was superimposed on a tv screen, I couldn't understand why our home wasn't all green lawn and white wood. . . . I rejected what was at hand and emulated the voices of the poets . . . big, male voices . . . all wrong for me . . . it seems crazy, but . . . I had never felt my home, family, and neighborhood unique or worthy of writing about. (1987a, 72)

Even though neither had Chicano/a literature to read as a child, both cite "reading voraciously" as a major factor in becoming writers. Anaya remembers Miss Pansy, the librarian who kept him supplied with books on Saturday afternoons which

> disappeared as the time of day dissolved into the time of distant worlds. . . . I took the time to read. . . . [T]hose of you who have felt the same exhilaration . . . will know about what I'm speaking. (1983, 306)

Anaya spent much time as well playing with friends, but Cisneros, being an only daughter in a family of six sons, was often lonely. She read, in part, to escape her loneliness. Cisneros reflects that her aloneness "was good for a would-be writer—it allowed . . . time to think . . . to imagine . . . to read and prepare" (1990, 256). Cisneros in "Notes to a Young(er) Writer" explains that her reading was an important "first step." She says she left chores undone as she was "reading and reading, nurturing myself with books like vitamins" (1987b, 74). Perhaps these experiences by Anaya and Cisneros nurtured their creation of protagonists who, like themselves, had no models—but were possessed by destiny, by inclination, and by courage to be artists—writers who would spin Chicano/a stories.

Bless Me, Ultima and *The House on Mango Street* are strong coming-of-age stories containing many of the elements of the traditional bildungsroman as well as other features that place them firmly in the Chicano/a tradition. The protagonists come of age by going through painful rites of passage, by performing heroic feats or passing tests with the help of mentors, by surviving symbolic descents into hell, and finally by reaching a new level of consciousness—the protagonists have changed and have moved from initial innocence to knowledge, from childhood to adolescence. Anaya's *Bless Me, Ultima* closely follows the traditional male bildungsroman. Its protagonist is the child, Antonio Márez; the novel begins when he says, "Ultima came to stay with us the summer I was almost seven" (1). Antonio, the first-person narrator, travels an almost classical mythic road, moving chronologically through his coming of age.

Cisneros' *House on Mango Street* is also narrated by a child protagonist. Esperanza, the protagonist, tells about her life on Mango Street; we see her family, friends, and community, their daily troubles and concerns. By the end of the story, she has gained understanding about both herself and her community/culture. But, unlike Anaya's chronological novel, *The House on Mango Street* is the story of growing awareness which comes in fits and starts, a series of almost epiphanic narrations mirrored in a structure that is neither linear nor traditional, a hybrid of fictive and poetic form, more like an impressionistic painting where the subject isn't clear until the viewer moves back a bit and views the whole. Esperanza tells her story in a series of forty-four, individually titled vignettes. Ellen McCracken believes that this bildungsroman, which she prefers to label a "collection" rather than a novel, "roots the individual self in a broader socio-political reality of the Chicano/a community" (1989, 64).

The settings of these two novels are very different— one essentially rural and the other urban—but each functions symbolically in the character's childhood and developing consciousness. In *Bless Me, Ultima,* Antonio lives on the edge of the llano, a wide open prairie, a place where his father's anarchic and noisy relatives and ancestors roamed as cowboys. The restlessness of his forebears is in Antonio's blood, and from the llano he learns about the wild forces of nature, herb lore, and the pagan awesomeness of the natural world. Through this landscape runs the river, heavily endowed with significance. Anaya has said that as a child in Santa Rosa, he spent much time by the river, his "numinous" place.

> I was haunted by the soul of the river. . . . [T]hat presence
> . . . touched my primal memory and allowed me to discover the river gods and the other essential symbols which were to become so important to my writing. (1977, 40)

But there are polarities even in the landscape in *Bless Me, Ultima,* for Antonio lives close to town, and he must try to learn the lessons of his schooling and the teachings of the Catholic Church. He must also try to understand the sometimes violent, sometimes despairing lives and compulsions of the people who live in the town. And there is yet a third place of importance to Antonio, El Puerto de Luna, the village of his mother, where the people are rooted, entrenched in agriculture and the land, moving quietly through life under the cycles of the moon. All these landscapes claim Antonio as a child, and he must decide upon their importance and allow or disallow their influences as he grows into adulthood.

For Esperanza in *The House on Mango Street,* the notion of "house"—or a space of her own—is critical to her coming of age as a mature person and artist. Ramón Saldívar says that this novel "emphasizes the crucial roles of racial and material as well as ideological conditions of oppression" (1990, 182). At the beginning of the novel, Esperanza explains how her parents talk about moving into a "real" house that "would have running water and pipes that worked" (Cisneros 1989, 4). Instead she lives in a run-down flat and is made to feel embarrassed and humiliated because of it. One day while she is playing outside, a nun from her school walks by and stops to talk to her.

> Where do you live? she asked.
> There, I said pointing to the third floor.
> You live *there?*
> *There.* I had to look to where she pointed—the third floor, the paint peeling, wooden bars Papa had nailed on the windows so we wouldn't fall out. You live *there?* The way she said it made me feel like nothing. (5)

Later in the novel, in a similar occurrence, a nun assumes that Esperanza lives in an even worse poverty-stricken area than, in fact, is the case. Julián Olivares says thus the "house and narrator become identified as one, thereby revealing an ideological perspective of poverty and shame" (1988, 162–63). Esperanza desires a space of her own, a real home with warmth and comfort and security, a home she wouldn't be ashamed of. For Esperanza, the house is also a necessity; echoing Virginia Woolf, she needs "A House of My Own" in order to create, a "house quiet as snow . . . clean as paper before the poem" (Cisneros 1989, 108).

Other houses on Mango Street do not live up to Esperanza's desires either, for they are houses that "imprison" women. Many vignettes illustrate this. There is the story of Marin who always has to baby-sit for her aunt; when her aunt returns from work, she may stay out front but not go anywhere else. There is also the story of Rafaela whose husband locks her indoors when he goes off to play dominoes. He wishes to protect his woman, his "possession," since Rafaela is "too beautiful to look at" (79). And there is Sally whose father "says to be this beautiful is trouble. . . . [H]e remembers his sister and is sad. Then she can't go out" (81). Sally marries, even before eighth grade, in order to escape the confinement and abuse of her father's house, but in the vignette, "Linoleum Roses," we see her dominated as well in the house of her husband.

> She is happy. . . . Except he won't let her talk on the telephone. And he doesn't let her look out the window. . . .
>   She sits home because she is afraid to go outside without his permission. (101–02)

Esperanza sees, as Olivares notes, that "the woman's place is one of domestic confinement, not one of liberation and choice" (163). And so, slowly, cumulatively, stroke by stroke, and story by story, Esperanza comes to realize that she must leave Mango Street so that she will not be entrapped by poverty and shame or imprisoned by patriarchy.

Another element of the bildungsroman is the appearance of a mentor who helps guide the protagonist. These coming-of-age novels both feature guides although they differ greatly in the two texts. In *Bless Me, Ultima,* we are introduced to Antonio's mentor, Ultima, in the very first line. Ultima, who comes to live with Antonio's family, is a wise woman, called a *curandera.* She is also a midwife, knowledgeable in healing and herb lore, and she possesses other, seemingly magic, shaman-like qualities: an owl "familiar" and the power to deal with the evil of witches (*brujas*). Antonio takes to her from the beginning. He says,

I was happy with Ultima. . . . [S]he taught me the names of plants and flowers . . . of birds and animals; but most important, I learned from her that there was beauty. . . . [M]y soul grew under her careful guidance. (14)

Beset by tensions and confusion in his world, Antonio turns increasingly to her.

In *The House on Mango Street* there is an ironic twist to the guidance of mentors, for often Esperanza is guided by examples of women she does *not* want to emulate, such as Sally and Rafaela. Esperanza's other mentors are very different from Ultima, but there are several role models who sometimes give her advice. They nurture her writing talent, show her ways to escape the bonds of patriarchy, and remind her of her cultural and communal responsibilities. Minerva is a young woman who, despite being married to an abusive husband, writes poems and lets Esperanza read them. She also reads Esperanza's writing. Aunt Lupe, dying of a wasting illness, urges Esperanza to keep writing and counsels her that this will be her freedom. Alicia, who appears in two stories, is, perhaps, the best role model. While she must keep house for her father, she still studies at the university so she won't be trapped. Alicia also reminds Esperanza that Esperanza *is* Mango Street and will one day return. McCracken says that Alicia fights "what patriarchy expects of her" and at the same time represents a clear-sighted, non-mystified vision of the barrio. . . . [S]he embodies both the antipatriarchal themes and the social obligation to return to one's ethnic community. (69–70)

The story, "Three Sisters," is a kind of subversive fairytale. Eperanza attends the wake of her friends' baby sister and is suddenly confronted by three mysterious old women. These women examine Esperanza's hand, tell her to make a wish, and advise, "When you leave, you must remember always to come back. . . . [Y]ou can't forget who you are. . . . [C]ome back for the ones who cannot leave as easily as you" (Cisneros 1989, 105). They direct her to remember her responsibilities to her community. In this bildungsroman, Esperanza is reminded consistently that the search for self involves more than mere personal satisfaction. All of these women offer guidance to help Esperanza in her coming of age.

The protagonists must endure other rites of passage to reach full personhood and understanding. Anaya's *Bless Me, Ultima* is deeply mythic. Part of Antonio's understanding comes from a series of ten dreams that Vernon Lattin believes are "just as important as Antonio's waking life. . . . [These] Jungian dreams help Antonio across the thresholds of transformation" (1979, 631). Antonio's first dream, for example, helps him with the anxiety he feels about the conflicting expectations that his father's and mother's families have for him. The dream is about his birth, and in it both families are at odds, battling with one another for control of Antonio's future. When the battle becomes so furious that guns are drawn, Ultima steps in and cries that only she will know his destiny. Antonio learns from this dream that he must not be destroyed by guilt or by the expectations of either family, but with Ultima he must find his one way in the world.

Near the end of the novel, Antonio experiences a terrifying, apocalyptic dream after witnessing the violent murder of Narcisco, who was coming to warn Ultima of danger. In the dream, Antonio sees his own death, and the blasphemous deaths of Ultima and the golden carp, symbol of the naturalistic, pagan world. All die and everything is destroyed; yet at the end it is decided that people will survive in "new form. . . . [There is] a new sun to shine its good light upon a new earth" (168). David Carrasco, who believes that *Bless Me, Ultima* can be read as a "religious text," says that the message Antonio learns is "the pattern of death and rebirth, decay and regeneration" and that Antonio is consciously aware that the "integration of his diverse and conflicting elements and the cultivation of sacred forces within a human being can lead to a life full of blessings" (1982, 218).

Antonio endures rites of passage in his waking life as well: he sees the brutality of his schoolmates towards those who are different; he watches two people, Lupito and Narcisco, shot to death; he is with Ultima when she dies. Perhaps his descent into darkness, a traditional rite of passage, occurs when he goes with Ultima to help cure his Uncle Lucas, who is desperately ill because of an evil spell cast by the witch-like Tenorio sisters. Ultima battles this spell, using Antonio as a kind of medium to expel the evil. He is very sick, but both he and his uncle vomit poisonous bile and recover. In the middle of the novel, he realizes what

Ultima revealed earlier in a dream: "The waters are one, Antonio. . . . [Y]ou have been seeing only parts . . . and not looking beyond into the great cycle that binds us all" (113). And so, Antonio comes of age, having gone beyond the dualities in his life.

Esperanza's rites of passage speak not through myth and dreams, but through the political realities of Mango Street. She faces pain and experiences violence in a very different way. Her major loss of innocence has to do with gender and with being sexually appropriated by men. In the vignette, "The Family of Little Feet," Esperanza and her friends don high heels and strut confidently down the street. They are pleased at first with their long legs and grown-up demeanors, then frightened as they are leered at, yelled to, threatened, and solicited. McCracken says, "Cisneros proscribes a romantic or exotic reading of the dress-up episode, focusing instead on the girls' discovery of the threatening nature of male sexual power" (67).

Perhaps Esperanza's "descent into darkness" occurs in the story "Red Clowns." Unlike the traditional bildungsroman, the knowledge with which she emerges is not that of regeneration, but of painful knowledge, the knowledge of betrayal and physical violation. In this story, she is waiting for Sally, who is off on a romantic liaison. Esperanza, all alone, is grabbed and raped. Afterward, she says, "Sally, make him stop. I couldn't make them go away. I couldn't do anything but cry. I don't remember. It was dark . . . . [P]lease don't make me tell it all" (Cisneros 1989, 100). In this story, Esperanza is also angry and calls Sally "a liar" because through books and magazines and the talk of women she has been led to believe the myth of romantic love. María

Herrera-Sobek calls this story a "diatribe" that is directed not only at Sally,

> but at the community of women in a conspiracy of silence . . . silence in not denouncing the "real" facts of life about sex and its negative aspects in violent sexual encounters, and *complicity* in romanticizing and idealizing unrealistic sexual relations. (177–78)

Esperanza, triply marginalized by race, class, and gender, has lost her innocence. Yet, despite this pain and violation, she manages to tell her story. She has come of age, and she understands that in the future she must serve *both* herself and her community.

> I will say goodbye to Mango. . . . Friends and neighbors will say, What happened to that Esperanza? . . . They will not know I have gone away to come back. For the ones I left behind. For the ones who cannot get out. (Cisneros 1989, 110)

And so, these two novels are every bit as strong, as literary, and as meaningful as the bildungsromans traditionally read in United States-literature classes. At the same time, they take different paths, preventing a single or stereotyped view of the Chicano/a coming-of-age experience. *Bless Me, Ultima* celebrates a rich cultural past and heritage, taking joy in myth and in the spiritual quest. *The House on Mango Street*, instead, celebrates the search for the real self and cultural responsibility in the face of different oppressions. Yet both texts show that Chicano/a literature has come of age; they announce "I am." That announcement should not go unheard.

Works Cited

Anaya, Rudolfo A. 1983. "In Commemoration: One Million Volumes." *American Libraries* 14.5 (May): 304–07.

———. 1977. "A Writer Discusses His Craft." *The CEA Critic* 40 (Nov.): 39–43.

———. 1972. *Bless Me, Ultima*. Berkeley, CA: Tonatiuh Quinto Sol International Publishers.

Bruce-Novoa, Juan. 1980. *Chicano Authors: Inquiry by Interview*. Austin: U of Texas P.

Carrasco, David. 1982. "A Perspective for a Study of Religious Dimensions in Chicano Experience: *Bless Me, Ultima* as a Religious Text." *Aztlan* 13 (Spring/Fall): 195–221.

Cisneros Sandra. 1990. "Only Daughter." *Glamour* (Nov.): 256, 285.

———. 1989. *The House on Mango Street*. New York: Vintage.

———. 1987a. "From a Writer's Notebook: Ghosts and Voices: Writing from Obsession." *The Americas Review* 15.1 (Spring): 69–73.

———. 1987b. "Notes to a Young(er) Writer." *The Americas Review* 15.1 (Spring): 74–76.

Herrera-Sobek, María. 1988. "The Politics of Rape: Sexual Transgression in Chicana Fiction." *The Americas Review* 15.3-4 (Fall-Winter): 17–82.

Lattin, Vernon E. 1979. "The Quest for Mythic Vision in Contemporary Native American and Chicano Fiction." *American Literature* 50.4 (Jan.): 625–40.

McCracken, Ellen. 1989. "Sandra Cisneros' *The House on Mango Street*: Community-Oriented Introspection and the Demystification of Patriarchal Violence." *Breaking Boundaries: Latina Writings and Critical Readings*. Ed. Asunción Horno-Delgado et al. Amherst: U of Massachusetts P. 62–71.

Olivares, Julián. 1988. "Sandra Cisneros' *The House on Mango Street* and the Poetics of Space." *Chicana Creativity and Criticism: Charting New*

Frontiers in American Literature. Ed. María Herrera-Sobek and Helena María Viramontes. Houston, TX: Arte Publico P. 160–69.

Saldívar, Ramón. 1990. *Chicano Narrative: The Dialectics of Difference*. Madison: U of Wisconsin P.

Dianne Klein, 1992. "Coming of Age in Novels by Rudolfo Anaya and Sandra Cisneros." *English Journal* 81.5 (September): 21–26. Reprinted with permission.

▪ ▪ ▪ ▪ ▪ ▪ ▪ ▪ ▪ ▪ ▪ ▪ ▪ ▪ ▪ ▪ ▪

Having Students Take a Critical Stance toward the Work of Sandra Cisneros

Suggested Essay Topics

■ Have students read a collection of poems by Sandra Cisneros to look for common themes. Ask them to write an essay exploring one of the themes they have discovered, including a discussion of why they think this theme is important to Cisneros and why they think it is relevant to her readers.

■ How is the structure of *The House on Mango Street* circular? Have students write an essay in which they explore how the structure of the novel reflects its theme.

■ Ask bilingual students to compare Sandra Cisneros's Spanish translation of "Good Hotdogs" with the original version in English. This poem can be found in the collection *Cool Salsa: Bilingual Poems on Growing Up Latino in the United States*, edited by Lori M. Carlson.

- Have students read *Nilda* by Nicholasa Mohr and write an essay comparing this 1973 story of a Puerto Rican girl living in the barrio of New York City during World War II with Sandra Cisneros's *The House on Mango Street.*

- In 1983, when *The House on Mango Street* was first published, stringent U.S. immigration laws limited the number of Mexicans who were allowed to immigrate to the United States. Have students research current immigration laws and write about how these laws affect the children of those who enter this country either legally or illegally.

- Have students read the short story "Eleven" from Sandra Cisneros's collection *Woman Hollering Creek and Other Stories.* Ask them to write an essay comparing the narrative voice in this piece with the narrative voice of Esperanza in *The House on Mango Street.*

- Outline the features of a hero's quest as described by Joseph Campbell in *The Hero with a Thousand Faces.* Ask students to write an essay comparing Esperanza in *The House on Mango Street* with classical heroes from mythology. How is the thing she seeks something of value for her culture? Where does she demonstrate her noble spirit? How is her journey essentially a search for herself?

- Sandra Cisneros is considered a feminist writer. Have students research what this label means and then ask them to find examples from Cisneros's poetry, essays, and fiction that offer evidence of her views regarding the role of women in society. Read Virginia Woolf's "A Room of One's Own" and compare this essay with Esperanza's desire for a place of her own in which to write.

■ Compare *The House on Mango Street* with other coming-of-age stories such as *Donald Duk* by Frank Chin, *Bless Me, Ultima* by Rudolfo Anaya, *A Tree Grows in Brooklyn* by Betty Smith, *Cold Sassy Tree* by Olive Ann Burns, *Bastard Out of Carolina* by Dorothy Allison, *Dreaming in Cuban* by Cristina Garcia, or *Yo!* by Julia Alvarez.

7 *Woman Hollering Creek* and More

Sandra Cisneros has said of her collection *Woman Hollering Creek and Other Stories* that her intent was to write stories that don't get told, stories of women who don't have the ability to document their lives. As she worked, she felt like a cartographer trying to chart new territory.

Warning

Do not even think of assigning *Woman Hollering Creek and Other Stories* to students unless you have read it from cover to cover. While the grouping of stories in Part I, "My Lucy Friend Who Smells Like Corn," will seem familiar territory to any student who has read *The House on Mango Street,* later stories deal with increasingly mature themes, specifically sex and sexual power. You know your students. You know your school culture. You know your community. The literary merit of the book is not in question. What may be is the appropriateness of this text for a particular group of students. At my school, we use *Woman Hollering Creek* in a Latino literature senior elective. I teach in liberal Santa Monica and I still think the book would be an unwise choice for ninth-grade literature circles following the study of *The House on Mango Street.*

The problem is that even when you win a censorship battle, you lose. The time involved in defending your right to teach a book and your students' right to read is time that could be much better spent. Of course, some battles must be fought, and I firmly agree with the NCTE/International Reading Association statement of intellectual freedom:

> All students in public school classrooms have the right to materials and educational experiences that promote open inquiry, critical thinking, diversity in thought and expression, and respect for others. Denial or restriction of this right is an infringement of intellectual freedom. (*Common Ground* [pamphlet])

What you don't want is to face a censorship challenge on a book that you haven't read. It happens, particularly with young teachers who remember reading and liking a book in college and assign the text to students without rereading it through teachers' eyes. You may need to be prepared to defend the use of graphic language in some of the later stories in *Woman Hollering Creek*.

If you are ever involved in a censorship dispute, the National Council of Teachers of English is there to support you. Just visit their Web site at www.ncte.org for the link on censorship. NCTE offers immediate advice, helpful documents, and other support at no cost to K–12 teachers, schools, and districts faced with challenges to literary works, films and videos, or teaching methods. Leave a message at 1-800-369-6283, ext. 3848, or call Charles Suhor, NCTE/SLATE field representative, directly at 334-280-4758. You can also use the form right on the Web page to report a challenge.

"Woman Hollering Creek," the Story

This powerful short story tells the tale of Cleófilas, a romantic young Mexican woman who marries a Texan, Juan Pedro, and moves across the border to the United States. There she suffers from isolation as well as from abuse by her husband. The story's title is the name of a creek that runs behind her house. La Gritona (Woman Hollering) originates in the legend of La Llorona, an important figure in Hispanic folklore. According to legend, La Llorona was the lover/wife of a man with whom she bore several children. When the man left her for a wife/mistress—you know how folktales have many versions—the woman throws her children into a stream, killing them, and then drowns herself. In the afterlife, she is told that she cannot rest until she finds her children. Ever since, the young mother La Llorona roams the banks of streams, weeping and calling out for her children.

I have the luxury of being able to ask my students to retell this folktale for others who have never heard it. What few of these Californians know, however, is that Woman Hollering Creek is an actual body of water just east of San Antonio where Interstate 10 crosses a small stream. I remind them that Sandra Cisneros herself lived in San Antonio.

My students are also able to help one another with the Spanish words that Cisneros sprinkles throughout the story.

Spanish Vocabulary from the Short Story "Woman Hollering Creek"

en el otro lado: on the other side

telenovela: soap opera

tú o nadie: you or no one

farmacía: pharmacy

La Gritona: woman hollering

arroyo: stream

"Pues, allá de los indios, quién sabe": "that came from the indians, who knows?"

entiendes?: understand?

consentida: princess

zócalo: big block on which a statue is placed

mi'hita: short for mi hijita, my daughter

"No es bueno para la salud. Mala suerte. Mal aire.": "It is not good for the health. Bad luck. Bad air."

La Llorona: weeping woman

mi querida: my dear

Themes and Motifs in "Woman Hollering Creek"

Women's Silence: Cleófilas is a traditional Mexican wife, obedient to her husband even though he beats her. She is surprised when a modern health worker who is taking her away from this abusive relationship hollers in joy and power while crossing the creek. Class discussions about domestic abuse naturally develop. When Juan Pedro first hits Cleófilas, "she didn't cry out or try to defend herself" (47). Have students note the first time Cleófilas speaks in the story—when she asks her husband to take her to a prenatal clinic. Even in the doctor's office, Cleófilas doesn't tell her story but lets her tears and the black and blue marks speak for her.

Crossing Borders: This story is set in the borderland between Mexico and the United States, in a place where cultural boundaries overlap. Students will want to talk about what Juan Pedro expected of his Mexican wife and her powerlessness when isolated from her extended family. Did he consciously choose a woman who would be so powerless? Cleófilas romanticizes her new town in Texas and her new husband, believing that life on the other side of the border will be more glamorous. Careful readers will note that Juan Pedro's job and the house he brings Cleófilas to are not as ideal as the naive narrator describes.

Suffering for Love: Cleófilas has fed on a steady diet of romance through popular songs and melodramatic Mexican soap operas, *telenovelas*. Have students identify the archetypal characters and traditional plot lines of such stories. What is their effect on young women's perception of themselves and their relationships? Lost in the fantasy of *telenovelas,* Cleófilas and her girlfriends come to believe that "to suffer for love is good. The pain all sweet somehow" (45). Discuss why this is a dangerous belief for anyone.

Throughout the story, Cleófilas has identified with the heroines in her *telenovelas* and with the weeping woman, La Llorona. At the conclusion, she begins to identify instead with the young medical worker who hollers whenever she drives her pickup across Woman Hollering Creek. Felice gives Cleófilas a ride to the Greyhound station where Cleófilas can catch a bus back to her family in Mexico. In Spanish, *felice* means "happy." Discuss with students how Cleófilas has changed over the course of this story. Is this a happy ending? How does the creek represent the "road not taken" for Cleófilas?

Connecting Prose and Poetry

Sandra Cisneros's poem "His Story" provides an interesting extension of the themes in "Woman Hollering Creek." It is also an excellent vehicle for examining the ways in which artists use their own lives as fodder for their art. Cisneros was the only daughter in a family of six boys. In this autobiographical poem, she describes her status in a Mexican American family as seen from her father's point of view.

His Story
Sandra Cisneros

I was born under a crooked star.
So says my father.
And this perhaps explains his sorrow.

An only daughter
whom no one came for
and no one chased away.

It is an ancient fate.
A family trait we trace back
to a great aunt no one mentions.

Her sin was beauty.
She lived mistress.
Died solitary.

There is as well
the cousin with the famous
how shall I put it?
profession.

She ran off with the colonel.
And soon after,
the army payroll.

And, of course,
grandmother's mother
who died a death of voodoo.
There are others.

For instance,
my father explains,
in the Mexican papers

a girl with both my names

was arrested for audacious crimes
that began by disobeying fathers.

Also, and here he pauses,
the Cubano who sells him shoes
says he too knew a Sandra Cisneros
who was three times cursed a widow.

You see.
An unlucky fate is mine
to be born woman in a family of men.

Six sons, my father groans,
all home.
And one female,
gone.

I ask students to read the poem and then ask them if their parents ever tell them stories about other teenagers who have gone "wrong" as a warning. Last year we had recently read Maxine Hong Kingston's *Woman Warrior* together, and several students immediately saw the connection between Kingston's mother's story about No Name Woman and Cisneros's father's story about "a girl with both my names." Students love talking analytically about their parents in this way. I push them to consider whether this is truly "His Story" (history?) or *her* story, that is, Sandra Cisneros's.

Further Resources

■ The Lannan Foundation has available a videotape of Sandra Cisneros giving a reading in Los Angeles on October 8, 1996, the year she won a Lannan award for fiction.

■ Both Barbara Kingsolver and Bebe Moore Campbell wrote book reviews for *Woman Hollering Creek* when it first appeared.

Kingsolver's was titled "Poetic Fiction with a Tex-Mex Tilt" and appeared in the *Los Angeles Times Book Review* on April 28, 1991. Campbell's was called "Crossing Borders" and appeared in the *New York Times Book Review* on May 26, 1991.

■ For more scholarly essays on *Woman Hollering Creek*, see Harryette Mullen's "A Silence between Us Like a Language: The Untranslatability of Experience in Sandra Cisneros's 'Woman Hollering Creek'" in *Melus* 21.2 (1996): 3–2, and Jean Wyatt's "On Not Being La Malinche: Border Negotiations of Gender in Sandra Cisneros's 'Never Marry a Mexican' and 'Woman Hollering Creek,'" *Tulsa Studies in Women's Literature* 14.2 (1995): 243–72.

Chronology of Sandra Cisneros's Life

■ ■

1954   Born on December 20 in Chicago, Illinois.

1966   Sandra Cisneros's parents buy their first house on the
            1500 block of N. Campbell Avenue in Chicago.

1972   Cisneros enrolls at Loyola University.

1976   After graduating from Loyola, Cisneros begins the Uni-
            versity of Iowa Writers' Workshop M.F.A. program in
            creative writing.

1978   Cisneros writes a master's thesis titled "My Wicked
            Wicked Ways" and receives her M.F.A. She begins
            working on the sketches that will later become *The
            House on Mango Street.*

1978–   Cisneros works at the Latino Youth Alternative High
1982   School in Chicago.

1980   First collection of poems, *Bad Boys,* is published

1982   Cisneros receives her first National Endowment of the
            Arts grant and leaves Chicago for Massachusetts to fin-
            ish *The House on Mango Street.*

1984   Arte Público Press publishes *The House on Mango Street.*

1985   *The House on Mango Street* receives the Before Columbus Foundation American Book Award.

1987   Third Woman Press publishes *My Wicked Wicked Ways,* a collection of poems. Cisneros is a visiting professor at California State University, Chico and receives a second NEA grant.

1991   Random House publishes the collection of short stories *Woman Hollering Creek.* Cisneros receives a Lannan Literary Award. *The House on Mango Street* is bought and reprinted by Vintage Books.

1994   *Loose Woman,* a collection of poetry, is published by Random House.

1995   Cisneros receives a MacArthur Fellowship. A translation of *The House on Mango Street (La casa en Mango Street)* by Elena Poniatowska is published by Random House.

1997   Father dies.

2002   Novel *Caramelo* published.

Works Cited

Beck, Isabel L., Margaret G. McKeown, Rebecca L. Hamilton, and Linda Kucan. 1997. *Questioning the Author: An Approach for Enhancing Student Engagement with Text.* Newark, DE: International Reading Association.

Benson, Sheila. "From the Barrio to the Brownstone." 1991. *Los Angeles Times* (May 7): F1.

Cazden, Courtney. 1988. *Classroom Discourse: The Language of Teaching and Learning.* Portsmouth, NH: Heinemann.

Chavez, Andrew. "Sandra Cisneros." 1993. *Notable Hispanic American Women,* ed. Diane Telgen and Jim Kamp. Detroit: Gale Research. 99–110.

Cisneros, Sandra. 1987. "Ghosts and Voices: Writing from Obsession." *The Americas Review* 15 (Spring): 45–49.

———. 1987. *My Wicked Wicked Ways.* New York: Turtle Bay.

———. 1987. "Notes to a Young(er) Writer." *The Americas Review* 15 (Spring): 110–17.

———. 1991. *The House on Mango Street.* New York: Vintage Contemporaries.

———. 1991. *Woman Hollering Creek and Other Stories.* New York: Random House.

———. 1993. "Who Wants Stories Now?" *The New York Times* (April 14): sec. 4, p. 17.

———. 1999. "Foreword." Pp. ix–xii in *Holler If You Hear Me: The Education of a Teacher and His Students,* Gregory Michie. New York: Teachers College Press.

ELIOT, T. S. 1930. "Little Gidding." V: 239–42 in *Four Quartets*. New York: Harcourt, Brace & World.

JASNA. 1993. "Letter from Sarajevo." *The NewYork Times* (April 9): A12.

JUSSAWALLA, FEROZA, and REED WAY DASENBROCK. 1992. *Interviews with Writers of the Post-Colonial World*. Jackson: University Press of Mississippi.

KLEIN, DIANNE. 1992. "Coming of Age in Novels by Rudolfo Anaya and Sandra Cisneros." *English Journal* 81 (September): 21–26.

MARTINEZ, RICK. 1995. "Geniuses Can Come in Many Colors." *Houston Chronicle* (November 12): F1.

MATCHIE, THOMAS. 1995. "Literary Continuity in Sandra Cisneros's *The House on Mango Street*." *The Midwest Quarterly* 37 (Autumn): 67–69.

RODRIGUEZ ARANDA, PILAR E. 1988. "On the Solitary Fate of Being Mexican, Female, Wicked, and Thirty-three: An Interview with Sandra Cisneros." *The Americas Review* 19: 68.

ROSENBLATT, LOUISE M. 1983. *Literature as Exploration*. New York: Modern Language Association.

SARBANES, JANET. 1997. Essay in *Novels for Students. Volume 2: Presenting Analysis, Context and Criticism on Commonly Studied Novels,* ed. Diane Telgen, Kevin Hile, Marie Rose Napierkowski, and Sheryl Ciccarelli. Detroit: Gale Research. 123–26.

SHEA, RENÉE. 1997. "Sandra Cisneros: Interview by Renée H. Shea." *The Bookwoman* 60 (Winter): 1–5.

TABOR, MARY B. W. 1993. "A Solo Traveler in Two Worlds." *The New York Times* (January 7): C1.

Author

Carol Jago teaches English at Santa Monica High School in Santa Monica, California, and directs the California Reading and Literature Project at UCLA. She is editor of *California English*, the quarterly journal of the California Association of Teachers of English (CATE). Jago has written a weekly education column for the *Los Angeles Times*, and her essays have appeared in *English Journal*, *Language Arts*, *NEA Today*, *GOAL Magazine*, *The Christian Science Monitor*, and other newspapers across the nation. She has served as director of the NCTE Commission on Literature and currently is a member of NCTE's Secondary Section. NCTE has published her first two volumes in this series, *Nikki Giovanni in the Classroom: "The same ol' danger but a brand new pleasure"* and *Alice Walker in the Classroom: "Living by the Word."* She is also the author of *With Rigor for All: Teaching the Classics to Contemporary Students*, *Beyond Standards: Excellence in the High School English Classroom*, and *Cohesive Writing: Why Concept Is Not Enough.*

This book was composed by Electronic Imaging.

The typefaces used on the cover include Arquitectura,
Zurich Ex Bt, Lucida Sans, and Helvetica.

The book was printed on 50-lb. Williamsburg Offset by Versa Press.